Excel 365 Advanced Topics

Leverage More Powerful Tools to
Enhance Your Productivity

Nathan George

Excel 365 Advanced Topics

Published 2023.

Published by GTech Publishing.

ISBN: 978-1-915476-09-8

Contents

Introduction

Excel 365 Advanced Topics covers a selection of topics that will enable you to take advantage of more powerful features in Excel in creating quick and flexible solutions for your data. My *Excel 2022 Basics* book covered the essentials of Excel and how to use Excel tools to create solutions for common Excel tasks. *Excel 365 Advanced Topics* does not rehash the content of that book. Rather, it goes beyond the basics and covers intermediate to advanced topics. This book aims to provide you with tools and techniques to solve data challenges requiring more than just a basic knowledge of Excel.

With *Excel 365 Advanced Topics*, you'll learn how to use features that make Excel one of the best data processing and analysis tools available today. The topics covered include automating Excel tasks with macros, creating data projections with What-If Analysis, analyzing large data sets with pivot tables and charts, creating conditional formulas with advanced logical functions, consolidating data from different worksheets, troubleshooting formula errors, and more. Unlike many other books, this book does not only show you how to use specific features but also in what context those features need to be used.

Who Is This Book For?

Excel 365 Advanced Topics is for you if you want to gain skills beyond the basics and become an Excel power user. In this book, you'll learn how to use some of the more powerful tools to address complex tasks and produce quicker results. This is not an exhaustive guide on advanced Excel but a selection of intermediate to advanced topics relevant to real-world productivity tasks you're more likely to encounter in your job or business.

This book assumes you have some basic knowledge of Excel. For brevity, *Excel 365 Advanced Topics* does not cover introductory topics already covered in my *Excel 2022 Basics* book (unless necessary for the lesson flow). If you need to brush up on the basics (or if you're new to Excel), then my *Excel 2022 Basics* book covers all the fundamentals you need.

Excel Versions

Excel for Microsoft 365 is the version of Excel that comes with a Microsoft 365 subscription, while Excel 2021 is the latest standalone (perpetual license) version in Office 2021. In the last few years, Microsoft has adopted a release cycle where new features are released for Microsoft 365 products as they become available. Conversely, standalone versions get new features approximately every 2-3 years when a new version of Office is released. This book covers the latest version of Excel for Microsoft 365 (2023 update) and Excel 2021.

How to Use This Book

This book can be used as a step-by-step training guide or a reference manual that you come back to from time to time. You can read it cover to cover or skip to certain parts that cover topics you want to learn. Although the chapters have been organized logically, the book has been designed to enable you to read a chapter as a standalone tutorial to learn how to carry out a certain task.

There are many ways to perform the same task in Excel. So, for brevity, this book focuses on the most efficient way of carrying out a task. However, alternative ways to perform a task are also provided occasionally.

As much as possible, the menu items and commands mentioned are bolded to distinguish them from the other text. This book also includes many screenshots to illustrate the covered features and tasks.

Assumptions

When writing this book, the software assumptions are that you already have Excel for Microsoft 365 (or the standalone version, Excel 2021) installed on your computer and that you're working on the Windows 11 (or Windows 10) platform.

If you are using an older version of Excel, you can still use this book (as long as you're aware that some of the covered features may be unavailable in your version). Alternatively, you can get my *Excel 2019 Advanced Topics* book, the previous edition of this book.

If you are using Excel on a Mac, simply substitute any Windows keyboard commands mentioned in the book for the Mac equivalent. All the features within Excel remain the same for both platforms.

If you're using Excel on a tablet or touchscreen device, simply substitute any keyboard commands mentioned in the book with the equivalent on your touchscreen device.

Practice Files

Downloadable Excel files have been provided to save you time if you want to practice in Excel as you follow the examples in the book. All examples are fully detailed in the book, and these files have been provided to save you the time it would take to create them, so they're optional. You can practice by changing the data to view different results. Please note that practice files have only been included for chapters where the examples use a sizable amount of sample data. Click the link below to go to the download page:

https://www.excelbytes.com/excel-365-at-download

Notes:
- Type the URL in your Internet browser's address bar, and press Enter to go to the download page. If you encounter an error, double-check that you have correctly entered all the URL characters.

- The files have been zipped into one download. Windows 10 (or Windows 11) has the functionality to unzip files. If your OS does not have this functionality, you'll need software like WinZip or WinRAR to unzip the file.

- The files are Excel files, so you will need to have Excel installed on your computer to open and use these files (preferably Excel 2013 and above).

- If you encounter any problems downloading these files, please contact me at **support@excelbytes.com**. Include the title of this book in your email, and the practice files will be emailed directly to you.

Chapter 1

Working with Multiple Workbooks

In this chapter, we will cover how to:

- Switch between multiple open workbooks.

- View multiple workbooks side-by-side.

- Arrange all open workbooks on your screen.

- Split the screen of your worksheet.

- Move data between workbooks.

- Move worksheets between workbooks.

There are occasions when you need to work with several open workbooks, and Excel provides features that make it easier to work with multiple windows.

Managing Multiple Windows

To work with multiple workbooks, open the main workbook and all the others.

Switch Between Workbooks

To switch between workbooks, do the following:

1. On the **View** tab, in the **Window** group, click **Switch Windows**.

2. Select the workbook you want to switch to from the dropdown list.

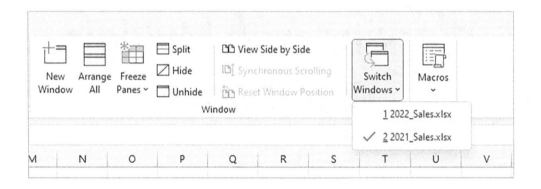

View Side-By-Side

To view worksheets from the different workbooks simultaneously, you can manually arrange them on your desktop or use an Excel command to tile them automatically.

To arrange two workbooks side by side, do the following:

1. In one of the workbooks, click the **View** tab. In the **Windows** group, click the **View Side by Side** button (if you have more than one workbook open, the **View Side by Side** command will be enabled).

If you have only two workbooks open, Excel will place the last one you opened above the earlier one.

If you have more than two workbooks open, Excel will display the **Compare Side by Side** dialog so that you can select which workbook to display alongside the active workbook.

2. Select the workbook you want to display alongside the active workbook and click **OK**.

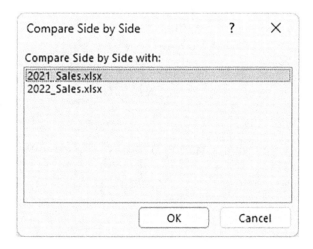

3. You can toggle the **View Side by Side** button to switch between a full screen of the active workbook and two workbooks.

Arrange All

The example above showed how to compare two workbooks side by side. Use the **Arrange All** command to compare more than two workbooks on your screen.

To view two or more workbooks on your desktop side by side, do the following:

1. Open the workbooks you want to view side by side.

2. On the **View** tab of one of the workbooks, click the **Arrange All** button.

   Excel displays the **Arrange Windows** dialog box, which has the options **Tiled**, **Horizontal**, **Vertical**, and **Cascade**.

3. Select the option you want, ensuring **Windows of Active Workbook** is unchecked.

4. Click **OK**.

New Window

Sometimes, you may want to view and work with worksheets in the same workbook in different windows.

To open a worksheet in a new Excel window, do the following:

1. Select the worksheet you want to view in a different window (click the worksheet tab).

2. On the **View** tab, in the **Window** group, click the **New Window** button.

3. Excel opens a new window of the same workbook (note that a new file is not created).

4. On the **View** tab, in the **Window** group, click the **Arrange All** button.

Excel displays the **Arrange Windows** dialog box.

5. Under **Arrange**, select **Tiled** to tile the windows on your screen (or select your desired option).

6. Select the **Windows of active workbook** checkbox.

7. Click **OK**.

Excel arranges the windows of the same workbook side by side on your screen.

Split Screen

The split screen method allows you to split your worksheet so you can see different parts of the worksheet in the same window. This feature comes in handy when you have a large amount of data and want to see different parts of the worksheet while working on the data.

To split the screen of a worksheet, do the following:

1. On the **View** tab, in the **Window** group, click the **Split** button.

   A horizontal and vertical dividing line will split the screen into four parts, with a scroll bar for each part. You can adjust the position of these dividers with your mouse pointer, depending on how you want the layout.

2. To move a dividing line, for example, the horizontal divider, hover over the divider until it changes to a double-headed arrow. You can now move the divider up or down, depending on how you want to view the split screen. You can do the same for the vertical line.

Moving Data Between Workbooks

There are two ways you can copy or move data between open workbooks.

Method 1

1. Arrange the workbooks so that the worksheets you want to work with are visible side-by-side on the screen.

2. Select the data you want to move or copy in the source worksheet.

3. On the **Home** tab, in the **Clipboard** group, click the **Copy** button (or select Ctrl+C on your keyboard) to copy the data. To move data, click the **Cut** button (or select Ctrl+X on your keyboard).

4. On the destination worksheet, click the top leftmost cell of the area where you want to paste the data.

5. On the **Home** tab, in the **Clipboard** group, click **Paste** (or select Ctrl+V on your keyboard) to paste the data.

Method 2

The second method to move or copy data between workbooks is to drag and drop the data from one workbook to the other.

Use the following steps to drag and drop data between workbooks:

1. Select the data in the source worksheet.

2. Hover over the edge of the selected range until the mouse pointer changes to a crosshair. This is the move pointer in Excel (see image below).

$10,227	$8,343	$5,467	$9,002
$13,263	$10,201	$6,199	$12,083
$13,680	$9,565	$14,089	$6,906
$5,610	$6,557	$5,756	$9,387
$11,335	$6,363	$5,980	$12,584
$10,214	$5,270	$11,708	$7,479
$5,746	$8,398	$6,390	$8,263
$5,594	$11,446	$7,794	$5,736
$14,537	$11,826	$8,848	$9,674
$9,118	$5,774	$7,533	$11,096
$13,417	$12,864	$13,032	$10,514
$6,573	$8,805	$13,254	$9,397

3. Once the pointer has changed to a move pointer, click and drag the selection to the other worksheet window.

4. You'll see a rectangle at the destination worksheet window representing the area containing the data to be pasted. Drag it to the left topmost cell of the range where you want to place the data and release the mouse button.

Note To copy the data, rather than move it, hold down the **Ctrl** key as you drag the data across to the other window.

---

5. After you release the mouse button, you may get a prompt that says: *"There's a problem with the clipboard, but you can still paste your content within this workbook."* Just click **OK** to dismiss the prompt and complete the action.

Moving Worksheets Between Workbooks

There are two ways you can copy or move worksheets between open workbooks. You can copy the worksheet using the Move and Copy command or drag and drop worksheets between workbooks.

Method 1

To use the Move or Copy command to copy sheets between workbooks, do the following:

1. Open the source workbook (that contains worksheets to be moved or copied) and the destination workbook where the worksheets will go. You must open the source and destination files to copy or move worksheets between them.

2. On the **View** tab, use the **Arrange All** command to arrange the windows side-by-side, preferably using the **Vertical** option.

3. Select the source workbook to make it the active window.

4. Select the source sheet by clicking its tab at the bottom of the window (to select more than one worksheet, hold down the **Ctrl** key and click additional sheets).

5. On the **Home** tab, in the **Cells** group, click the **Format** button and select **Move or Copy Sheet** on the menu.

   Excel displays the **Move or Copy** dialog box.

6. In the **Move or Copy** dialog box, select the destination workbook in the **To book** dropdown list box.

7. Under **Before sheet**, select where to place the worksheet inside the destination workbook.

   To create a copy of the worksheet, rather than move it, select the **Create a copy** checkbox.

8. Click **OK** to complete the action.

Method 2

Just as you can copy data in a range between workbooks using drag-and-drop, you can also move or copy worksheets between workbooks using drag-and-drop.

To move or copy worksheets between workbooks using drag-and-drop, do the following:

1. Arrange the source and destination workbooks side-by-side to see both on the screen. You can do this manually or use the **Arrange All** command described above. Preferably you should arrange them vertically.

2. Click the sheet tab in the destination workbook to select the worksheet to be moved or copied (to select more than one sheet, hold down the **Ctrl** key and click additional sheets).

3. Drag the sheet from the source workbook to the destination workbook with your mouse. You'll see a little document icon representing the sheet you're moving.

> **📝 Note** To copy the sheet (instead of moving it), hold down the **Ctrl** key as you drag the sheet from the source workbook to the destination workbook. The document icon will include a plus symbol (+) to indicate the copy action.

4. You'll see a small arrow at the destination workbook indicating where the sheet would be placed. You can move this arrow left or right to choose where you want to place the sheet before releasing the mouse button to place the sheet there.

This method is a much faster way to move or copy worksheets between two open workbooks.

Chapter 2

Using External Data

This chapter covers the following:

- Importing data from a Microsoft Access database.

- Importing data from a delimited text file like a CSV file.

- Importing data from a website with constantly changing live data, for example, Forex data.

- Transforming imported data with the Power Query Editor.

When working with Excel, you often have situations when you have to import data from other applications. The most common are comma-separated files (CSV) or some other form of delimitation.

Importing Data from Microsoft Access

Follow the steps below to import data from an Access Database:

1. Open the workbook in which you want to import the data.

2. On the **Data** tab, in the **Get & Transform Data** group, click **Get Data**. Then select **From Database** > **From Microsoft Access Database**.

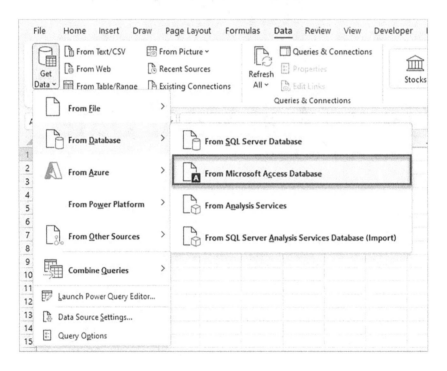

3. In the **Import Data** dialog box, navigate to the Access database (this will usually be an ACCDB or MDB file). Select the file and click the **Import** button. For this example, we're using the file **HighlandFurniture.accdb**.

   Excel displays the **Navigator** dialog box.

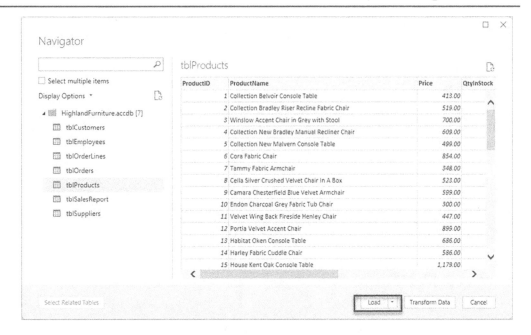

The Navigator dialog box is divided into two panes. The left pane displays a list of tables and queries from the data source. The right pane displays a preview of the fields and data in the selected item.

Note To import more than one table from the selected Access database, click the **Select Multiple Items** checkbox on the left pane. Excel will then display check boxes against each item on the list, which allows you to select more than one table from the list.

4. After selecting the table(s) to import, click the **Load** button.

Excel imports the data into a new worksheet as an Excel table (with table features).

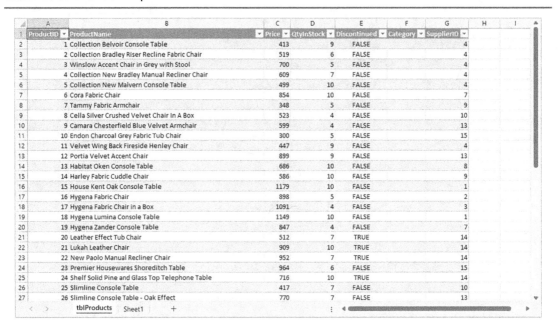

The Navigator dialog box also provides other options for uploading the Access data.

Transforming Data Before Importing

The **Transform Data** button is at the bottom of the Navigator dialog box. When you click this button, Excel opens the Excel **Power Query Editor**, which provides several tools to transform the data before it is imported. For example, you may want to import only some columns or only some of the rows.

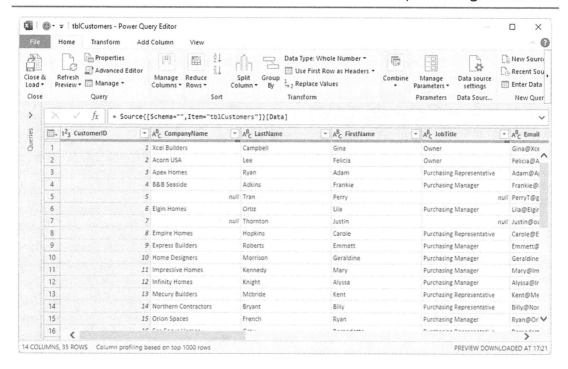

The Power Query Editor is covered in more detail in chapter 3.

Other Load Options

For more load options, at the bottom of the **Navigator** dialog, click the dropdown arrow on the **Load** button, then select **Load To** from the menu to open the **Import Data** dialog box.

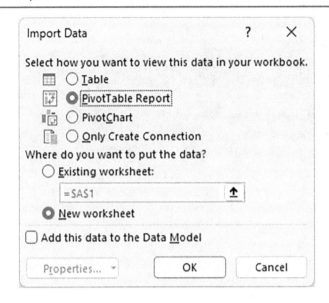

This dialog box allows you to import the Access data as:

- An Excel Table (default)

- A PivotTable

- A PivotChart

- Only a connection to the database.

You can also import the data into an **Existing worksheet** or a **New worksheet** (default).

Importing Text/CSV Files

As Excel stores data in cells, the text files you can import need to have a method of separating the values. The character that marks this separation is called a *delimiter* because it marks the "limit" of a value. The most common delimiter used for text files is the comma. For example, you may have a series of numbers [200, 400, 100, 900] representing data in four cells. The text files that use a comma as a delimiter are called comma-separated values (CSV) files.

Sometimes, text files use different delimiters when a comma might not be appropriate. For example, using a comma delimiter may present a problem for financial figures (like $100,000) because commas are part of the values. Hence, some financial data programs export their data by using the tab character as a delimiter, and these files are referred to as Tab-delimited files.

Follow the steps below to import a text data file into Excel:

1. Open the workbook in which you want to import the data.

2. On the **Data** tab, in the **Get & Transform Data** group, click the **From Text/CSV** button. Excel displays the **Import Data** dialog box.

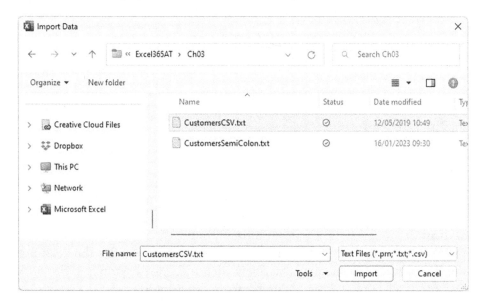

3. In the **Import Data** dialog box, navigate to the text or CSV file. Select the file and click the **Import** button. For this example, we're using **CustomersCSV.txt**.

Excel displays the Navigator dialog box.

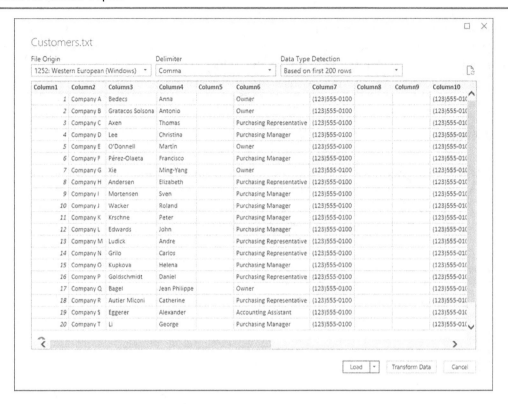

Excel examines the data in the text or CSV file and attempts to correctly split it into separate columns based on the delimiter it identifies as the separator.

4. **Delimiter box**: As shown in the image above, three boxes are at the top of the Navigator dialog box. The **Delimiter** dropdown list specifies the delimiter used in the text file. If this has been wrongly identified, for example, if your file is Tab delimited, select the correct delimiter from the dropdown list.

   Leave **File Origin** and **Data Type Detection** at their default values for anything other than complex data imports requiring advanced knowledge.

5. **Load option**: If Excel correctly parsed the data in your text file as shown in the Navigator's preview, you can select one of the following options to import the data into your worksheet.

   At the bottom of the dialog box, you have three options for uploading the data:

   ▪ The **Load** button imports the data, as seen in the Navigator preview, into your workbook (in a new worksheet).

- The **Load To** option (on the Load button's dropdown menu) gives you more options for how you want to import the data and where to place the data. The Load To dialog box is discussed above under importing data from Microsoft Access.

- The **Transform Data** button opens the data in the **Power Query Editor**. This enables you to query and transform the data before importing it. For example, you may want to import only a few columns in the data set or data that meet some criteria. Transform data allows you to remove the columns you don't want to import.

-☀️-**Tip** If the source table is not too large, you can also import the full data into Excel and delete the columns you don't want.

Using the Convert Text to Columns Wizard

Occasionally, Excel cannot correctly parse the data into separate columns even after you change the Delimiter, File Origin, and Data Type Detection. If Excel insists on importing each row as a single column, you can import the data and then use the **Text to Columns** tool to split the values into separate columns.

After importing the data into Excel, follow the steps below to split the data into separate columns:

1. In your worksheet, select the range containing the data that needs to be separated. For this example, we're using the file **TextToColumnsWizard.xlsx**.

2. On the **Data** tab, in the **Data Tools** group, click the **Text to Columns** button.

   Excel opens the **Convert Text to Columns Wizard** dialog box.

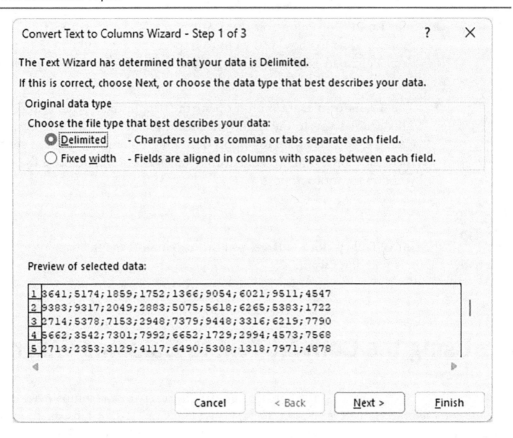

Convert Text to Columns Wizard - Step 1 of 3   ?   X

The Text Wizard has determined that your data is Delimited.

If this is correct, choose Next, or choose the data type that best describes your data.

Original data type

Choose the file type that best describes your data:

⦿ Delimited   - Characters such as commas or tabs separate each field.

◯ Fixed width   - Fields are aligned in columns with spaces between each field.

Preview of selected data:

```
1 3641;5174;1859;1752;1366;9054;6021;9511;4547
2 9383;9317;2049;2883;5075;5618;6265;5383;1722
3 2714;5378;7153;2948;7379;9448;3316;6219;7790
4 5662;3542;7301;7992;6652;1729;2994;4573;7568
5 2713;2353;3129;4117;6490;5308;1318;7971;4878
```

Cancel   < Back   Next >   Finish

3. On step 1 of the wizard, choose between **Delimited** and **Fixed width**, depending on how your data is separated. Then click the **Next** button to go to step 2.

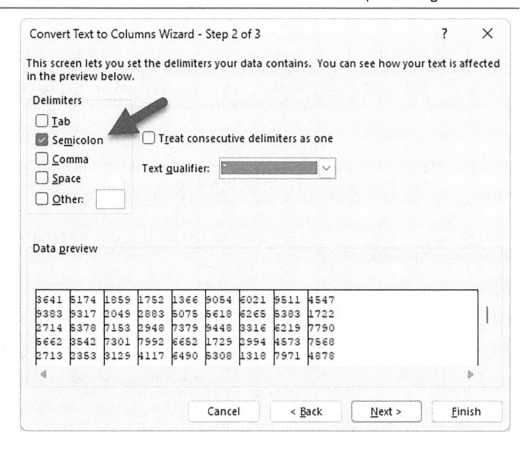

4. **Delimiters**: If you selected the Delimited option in Step 1 of the wizard, do one of the following in Step 2:

- Under the **Delimiters** section, select the delimiter for your text file. In our example above, the delimiter is a semicolon.

- Select **Other** if the delimiter in your text file is not one of the provided options. Then, enter the character in the text box next to Other.

- If your file uses more than one delimiter type, for example, a comma and a space, select all of them under Delimiters, including the **Treat Consecutive Delimiters As One** checkbox.

Fixed width files: If your file is a fixed-width separated file and you selected the Fixed width option in step 1 of the wizard, then in step 2, you'll see a preview that allows you to determine the column breaks by clicking in the text area to create column lines. You can drag and resize these column lines to match the column breaks in the text.

5. **Text Qualifier:** By default, the Convert Text to Columns Wizard treats characters enclosed in double quotes as text entries, not numbers. If your text file uses single quotes, then you would select it from the **Text Qualifier** dropdown list.

6. When you're happy with the preview of the text in step 2, click the **Next** button to go to step 3 of the wizard.

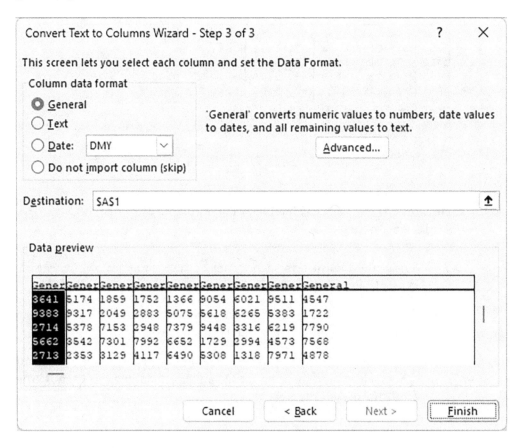

7. In step 3 of the process, you can click each column under **Data preview** and select different settings for importing the data in the top section (**Column data format**).

   You can choose between General (default), Text, and Date data formats. Alternatively, you can select **Do not import column (skip)** to skip importing that column.

   -ᗧ-**Tip** On some occasions, it would be faster to import the data using the **General** data format and then change the data format for the columns you want to change within Excel.

   ---

8. The **Destination** box shows you the top-leftmost cell of the range where the text will be placed. If you want it in a different part of the worksheet, select a different destination by clicking the Expand Dialog button (up arrow) on the right of the field.

9. Once you're done, click **Finish** to convert the data.

Excel splits the imported text file entries into separate columns in place of the previous data. You can now set the data format (if you didn't do that during the conversion) and adjust column widths.

-ᗧ-**Tip** You can directly open some CSV files in Excel and convert them to Excel workbooks. If CSV files are associated with Excel on your computer, you can double-click the file to open it in Excel. Alternatively, you can open the file from within Excel even if the CSV extension is not associated with Excel on your PC. Once the file is open in Excel and the data is displayed properly, you can then save the file as an Excel workbook.

Importing Data from a Website

To import data from the web, you must first identify the web address (URL) that contains the data you want to import. Then you can use the import tools in Excel to import the data directly from the webpage into your worksheet.

Let's say we want to import currency exchange rates from the web into our worksheet.

Below is how the data looks on the website after using our date criteria to select the records we want to see. We can now use this URL to import the data tables on the website.

https://www.xe.com/currencytables/?from=USD&date=2023-01-01#table-section

Currency Table: USD — US Dollar

All figures are mid-market rates, which are not available to consumers and are for informational purposes only.

Jan 1, 2023, 17:00 UTC

CURRENCY	NAME	UNITS PER USD	USD PER UNIT
USD	US Dollar	1	1
EUR	Euro	0.9343609460913234	1.0702502113163677
GBP	British Pound	0.82655869945566	1.2098354305127534
INR	Indian Rupee	82.7284215423729	0.012087744228116419
AUD	Australian Dollar	1.4676006339014427	0.6813842791424928
CAD	Canadian Dollar	1.353572833123755	0.7387855130722556

To import data from a website, do the following:

1. Identify the URL for the web page containing the table you want to import and copy it to the clipboard.

2. On the **Data** tab, in the **Get & Transform Data** group, click the **From Web** button. Alternatively, on the **Data** tab, select **Get Data** > **From Other Sources** > **From Web**.

   Excel displays the **From Web** dialog box.

3. Paste the web address containing the data you want to import in the **URL** box.

4. Click **OK** to establish a connection to the website.

Note If this is the first time you've connected to the website, Excel may display an **Access Web-content** dialog box with different connection options. Connect with the default, which is **Anonymous**.

   Once connected, Excel will display the **Navigator** dialog box, listing the data tables on the Selection pane on the left.

5. Select the required table on the left pane. You can preview the data on the right pane.

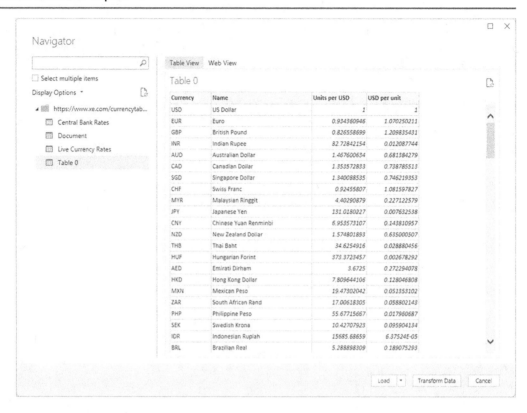

6. Click the **Load** button to import the data into a new worksheet in your workbook.

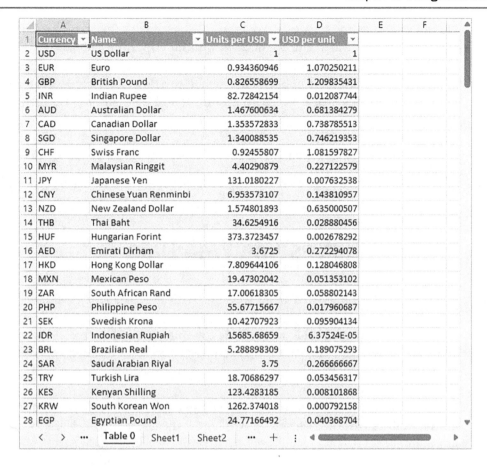

	A	B	C	D	E	F
1	Currency ▾	Name ▾	Units per USD ▾	USD per unit ▾		
2	USD	US Dollar	1	1		
3	EUR	Euro	0.934360946	1.070250211		
4	GBP	British Pound	0.826558699	1.209835431		
5	INR	Indian Rupee	82.72842154	0.012087744		
6	AUD	Australian Dollar	1.467600634	0.681384279		
7	CAD	Canadian Dollar	1.353572833	0.738785513		
8	SGD	Singapore Dollar	1.340088535	0.746219353		
9	CHF	Swiss Franc	0.92455807	1.081597827		
10	MYR	Malaysian Ringgit	4.40290879	0.227122579		
11	JPY	Japanese Yen	131.0180227	0.007632538		
12	CNY	Chinese Yuan Renminbi	6.953573107	0.143810957		
13	NZD	New Zealand Dollar	1.574801893	0.635000507		
14	THB	Thai Baht	34.6254916	0.028880456		
15	HUF	Hungarian Forint	373.3723457	0.002678292		
16	AED	Emirati Dirham	3.6725	0.272294078		
17	HKD	Hong Kong Dollar	7.809644106	0.128046808		
18	MXN	Mexican Peso	19.47302042	0.051353102		
19	ZAR	South African Rand	17.00618305	0.058802143		
20	PHP	Philippine Peso	55.67715667	0.017960687		
21	SEK	Swedish Krona	10.42707923	0.095904134		
22	IDR	Indonesian Rupiah	15685.68659	6.37524E-05		
23	BRL	Brazilian Real	5.288898309	0.189075293		
24	SAR	Saudi Arabian Riyal	3.75	0.266666667		
25	TRY	Turkish Lira	18.70686297	0.053456317		
26	KES	Kenyan Shilling	123.4283185	0.008101868		
27	KRW	South Korean Won	1262.374018	0.000792158		
28	EGP	Egyptian Pound	24.77166492	0.040368704		

‹ › ⋯ **Table 0** Sheet1 Sheet2 ⋯ + ⋮

Other Import Options

To import more than one table of data from the web page, select the **Select Multiple Items** check box and then click the checkboxes against the table names you want to import.

Once you've selected the table(s) you want to import on the page, you have the following three import options:

- **Load:** This option imports the data, as seen in the Navigator preview pane, into a new worksheet (as shown above).

- The **Load To** option (on the Load button's dropdown menu) opens the **Import Data** dialog box, giving you more options for importing the data and where to place it. You can import the data as a worksheet Table, PivotTable, or PivotChart. You can choose to establish a data connection without importing the data.

- The **Transform Data** button opens the data in the **Power Query Editor**, allowing you to query and transform it before importing it. For example, you may want to import only a subset of the data.

After importing the data, you can manipulate and work with the data as you would with any other Excel table.

Refreshing Web Data

When working with tables imported from websites with live data, for example, financial websites like the Nasdaq or Dow Jones (while the markets are still open), you can refresh the data to reflect any changes in the data. When you import the data, Excel automatically stores information about the connection, so you just need one button click to refresh the data.

To refresh data imported from a website, on the **Data** tab, in the **Queries & Connections** group, click the **Refresh All** button. Excel will automatically re-establish the connection and refresh the imported data with the latest data from the website. Alternatively, you can refresh the data anytime by right-clicking the table name in the **Queries & Connections** pane and selecting **Refresh** from the shortcut menu.

In the case of dynamic values that are constantly changing, it comes in handy to be able to refresh the values regularly without having to re-import the data.

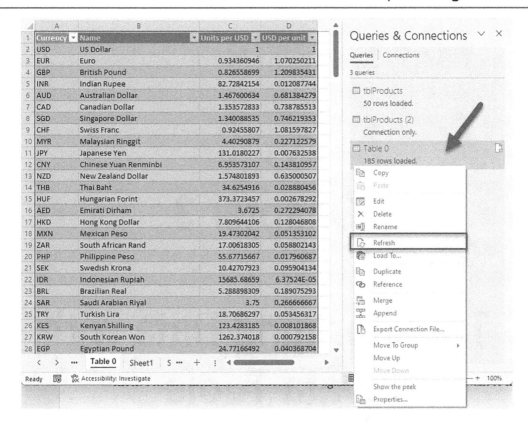

Other Database Sources

Apart from Microsoft Access, the **Get Data** command on the **Data** tab also enables you to import data from a variety of database sources, including:

- **From SQL Server Database:** This option enables you to import data from or create a connection to an SQL Server database.

- **From Analysis Services**: This option enables you to import data from an SQL Server Analysis cube.

- **From SQL Server Analysis Services Database (Import)**: This is to import data from an SQL Server database with the option to use an MDX or DAX query.

Chapter 3

Transforming Data with Data Tools

In this chapter we will cover how to:

- Find and remove duplicate rows in your data.
- Find and delete blank rows in your data.
- Convert text to columns.
- Consolidate data from different worksheets into one worksheet.

There are several data tools provided in Excel for Microsoft 365 you can use to quickly perform data organizing tasks. We'll cover the most common tasks where these tools are utilized in this chapter.

Removing Duplicates

On some occasions, you may have a data set, for example, a list of customers you want to use for a mail merge. You want to make sure that you don't have duplicate records before you start the mail merge process so that you don't send the mail to the same customer more than once.

To remove duplicate entries in a list, do the following:

1. Click any cell in the range.

2. On the **Data** tab, in the **Data Tools** group, click the **Remove Duplicates** button.

    Excel displays the **Remove Duplicates** dialog box.

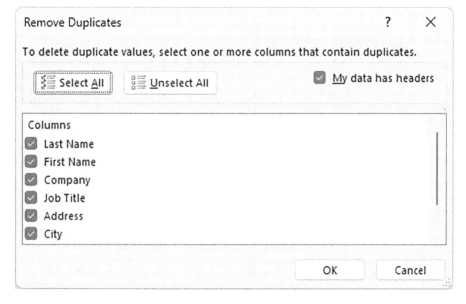

3. Leave all the columns selected (if you want the full row checked against one another) and click **OK**.

4. A message will be displayed telling you if any duplicates were found and how many records were deleted. Click **OK** to complete the process.

Note You may have cases where you only want to use a few columns to check for duplicate records. For example, you may have more than one person on your list from the same address, but you only want each address once for the mail merge. In cases like that, deselect all the other columns and only select the columns you want to use to check for duplicates.

Tip You can also use the Power Query Editor to remove duplicate rows. See the section **Delete Blank Rows** below for how to open and use the Power Query Editor to transform your data.

Deleting Blank Rows

There may be occasions when you have unnecessary blank rows in your data that you want to remove. If you have a large list with a lot of empty rows, it could be time-consuming to manually find and delete the empty rows. Fortunately, there are ways you can do this automatically. We will cover two methods for achieving this task here. The first method uses commands on the Excel ribbon and the second method involves using the Power Query Editor, which has a command for deleting blank rows.

Method 1

There is no direct command for deleting blank rows on the ribbon, but you can combine a couple of commands to achieve the task.

To delete blank rows, do the following:

1. Select the range that contains the blank rows.
2. On the **Home** tab, in the **Editing** group, click **Find & Select**.
3. Select **Go To Special** from the dropdown menu.
4. On the **Go To Special** dialog, select **Blanks** and click **OK**.

Excel will select the blank cells in the range.

5. On the **Home** tab, in the **Cells** group, select **Delete** > **Delete Sheet Rows**.

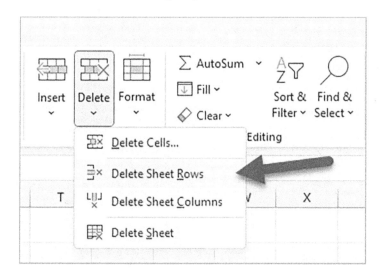

And that's it! Excel will delete all the rows that were identified and selected using the Go To Special command.

🔆**-Tip** If you delete any rows in error, you can undo your changes by clicking the **Undo** button on the **Home** tab to reverse your changes.

Method 2

The second method involves using the Power Query Editor in Excel.

To delete blank rows using the Power Query Editor, do the following:

1. Select the data list for which you want to remove blank rows.

🔆**-Tip** To quickly select a range, click the top-left cell of the range, hold down the **Shift** key, and click the bottom-right cell.

---

2. On the **Data** tab, in the **Get & Transform Data** group, click the **From Table/Range** command button.

Excel will open and display your data in the **Power Query Editor**, which is an add-on tool in Excel with a separate user interface and ribbon.

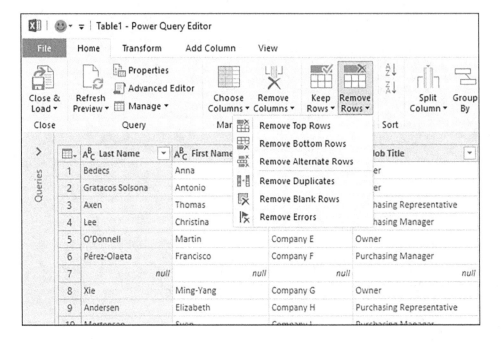

3. On the **Home** tab of the Power Query Editor, click the dropdown arrow on the **Remove Rows** command button, and select **Remove Blank Rows** from the dropdown menu.

Excel deletes all the blank rows identified in the data list.

4. To save your transformed data, on the **Home** tab of the Power Query Editor, click the **Close & Load** command button to paste the transformed data in a new sheet in your workbook and close the Power Query Editor.

That's it! Your data list without the blank rows will now be in a new sheet with the original data list unchanged. Note that, among many other actions, you can also use the Power Query Editor to remove duplicate rows.

Converting Text to Columns

If you work with a lot of data from different sources, there could be occasions where you receive a text file with values that are separated by commas. When you copy and paste the values in Excel, it would place them all in one column. You can separate these values into different columns using the text to columns command.

	A	B	C
1	**Name**	**Last Name**	**First Name**
2	Henderson, Bruce		
3	Anderson, Louis		
4	Foster, Earl		
5	Hill, Sean		
6	Martinez, Benjamin		
7	Perez, Joe		
8	Johnson, Shawn		
9	Roberts, Kenneth		
10	Martin, Cynthia		
11	Mitchell, Susan		
12			
13			

To convert delimited text values into separate columns, do the following:

1. Select the range containing the text you want to split.

2. On the **Data** tab, in the **Data Tools** group, click the **Text to Columns** button.

3. In the Convert Text to Columns Wizard, select **Delimited** and click **Next**.

4. Select the **Delimiters** for your data. For our example (in the image above), the delimiters are **Comma** and **Space**. You also have the options of Tab, Semicolon, and Other, which allows you to specify the delimiter if it's not one of the default options.

   The **Data preview** portion of the screen shows you a preview of how your data would look after the conversion.

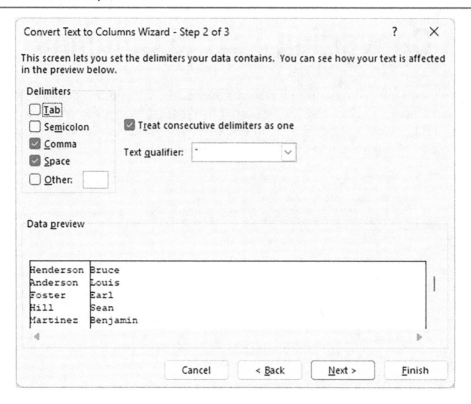

5. Click **Next**.

6. In Step 3 of the wizard, select the **Column data format** or use what Excel chooses for you.

7. In the **Destination** field, click the Expand Dialog button (up arrow), and on your worksheet, select the top leftmost cell where you want the split data to appear. The cell reference for the destination will be entered in the field.

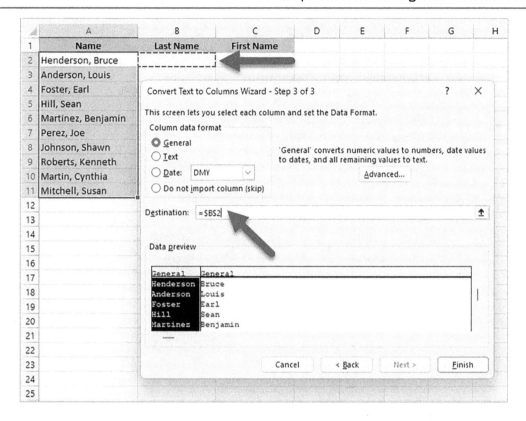

8. Click **Finish**.

The delimited text will now be split into different columns. You can delete the initial column with the original text from the worksheet or move it to another sheet if you intend to keep it.

	A	B	C	D
1	**Name**	**Last Name**	**First Name**	
2	Henderson, Bruce	Henderson	Bruce	
3	Anderson, Louis	Anderson	Louis	
4	Foster, Earl	Foster	Earl	
5	Hill, Sean	Hill	Sean	
6	Martinez, Benjamin	Martinez	Benjamin	
7	Perez, Joe	Perez	Joe	
8	Johnson, Shawn	Johnson	Shawn	
9	Roberts, Kenneth	Roberts	Kenneth	
10	Martin, Cynthia	Martin	Cynthia	
11	Mitchell, Susan	Mitchell	Susan	
12				
13				

Consolidating Data from Multiple Worksheets

Data consolidation provides an easy way to summarize data from multiple worksheets in a master worksheet. You can consolidate data from different worksheets in the same workbook, different workbooks, or a combination of both. The process allows you to select the ranges you want to add to the consolidation from different sources and Excel will aggregate the data in another workbook.

To consolidate data, all the ranges to be included in the consolidation must be of the same shape and size.

In the following example, we have sales data from 2020 to 2022 that we want to consolidate from three worksheets into one worksheet titled **Sales for 2020 - 2022**.

	A	B	C	D	E
1	Sales for 2020 - 2022				
2					
3		New York	Los Angeles	London	Paris
4	Jan				
5	Feb				
6	Mar				
7	Apr				
8	May				
9	Jun				
10	Jul				
11	Aug				
12	Sep				
13	Oct				
14	Nov				
15	Dec				

The three workbooks we will be consolidating the data from are:
- 2020_Sales.xlsx
- 2021_Sales.xlsx
- 2022_Sales.xlsx

To consolidate cell ranges from the three workbooks, do the following:

1. Open the destination workbook (the workbook into which you want to consolidate your data). In our example, it will be 2020_2022_Sales.xlsx.

2. Open the source workbooks (the workbooks with the data you want to consolidate). For this example, the source workbooks are the three workbooks listed above.

3. Switch back to the source workbook.

4. On the **Data** tab, in the **Data Tools** group, click the **Consolidate** button.

   Excel displays the **Consolidate** dialog box.

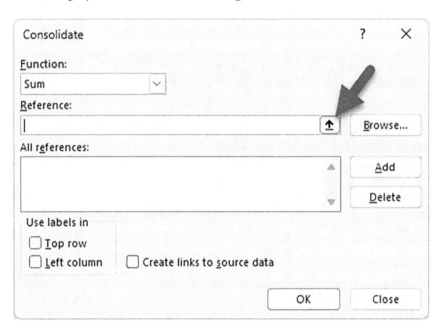

5. On the **View** tab, in the **Window** group, click **Switch Windows**. The menu has a list of all open workbooks.

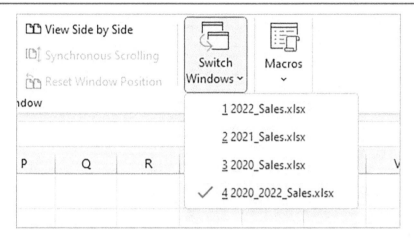

6. On the dropdown menu, select the first workbook containing data you want to consolidate. Excel makes this the active workbook. For our example, the first workbook is *2020_Sales.xlsx*.

7. In the Consolidate dialog box, click the **Reference** box, then select the cells you want to add to the consolidation on the worksheet. Excel adds a reference to the selected range to the Reference box.

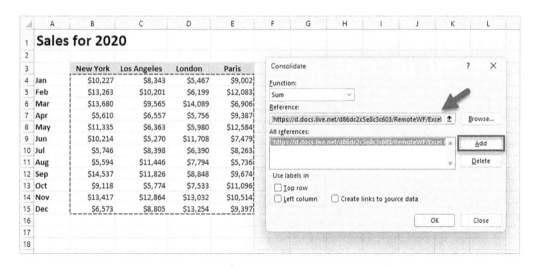

8. In the Consolidate dialog box, click the **Add** button to add the selected range to the **All references** box.

9. Repeat steps 5 to 8 above for any additional ranges containing data you want to consolidate. These ranges can come from different workbooks or different

worksheets in the same workbook. For this example, these would be from *2021_Sales.xlsx* and *2022_Sales.xlsx*.

10. **Function**: The default function Excel uses to aggregate the data in the consolidated worksheet is **Sum**. You can select a different function from the **Function** dropdown list, like Count or Average.

11. Click **OK** when you've added all the ranges to be consolidated.

	A	B	C	D	E
1	**Sales for 2020 - 2022**				
2					
3		**New York**	**Los Angeles**	**London**	**Paris**
4	Jan	$37,112	$37,034	$33,116	$28,834
5	Feb	$26,928	$31,263	$21,982	$33,483
6	Mar	$36,511	$28,649	$33,158	$28,713
7	Apr	$26,144	$20,178	$22,248	$24,655
8	May	$32,717	$29,072	$25,157	$29,413
9	Jun	$38,505	$22,090	$29,286	$35,879
10	Jul	$30,452	$35,911	$27,040	$24,865
11	Aug	$22,207	$32,373	$22,887	$32,187
12	Sep	$31,925	$36,538	$28,356	$27,973
13	Oct	$38,797	$24,493	$22,909	$32,532
14	Nov	$33,490	$33,315	$39,205	$35,915
15	Dec	$27,475	$34,710	$26,777	$29,943
16					

Each cell in the consolidated data will now hold the sum for that cell from all the consolidated worksheets.

Transforming Data with the Power Query Editor

The Power Query Editor enables you to transform external data in different ways before importing the data into Excel. For example, you may want to import data from an SQL Server table with several columns and hundreds of thousands of records. However, you only want to import a subset of the columns and rows. You could attempt to bring the full table into Excel and then remove the unwanted data, but for very large datasets, Excel may not be able to handle all the records. Also, it may be too cumbersome to bring all the records into Excel. In cases like these, you can use the Power Query Editor to query and return only the data you need from the external data source.

You can also use the Power Query Editor for advanced queries involving multiple tables linked by relationships. However, that level of coverage is outside the scope of this book. For basic data-transforming tasks, the Power Query Editor should be familiar to you as its interface and ribbon are not that dissimilar to Excel.

Example

The following example details how to import a subset of data from an Access database, **tblProducts**. We only want some of the columns and records for products that are not discontinued.

Open the destination workbook.

On the **Data** tab, in the **Get & Transform Data** group, select **Get Data** > **From Database** > **From Microsoft Access Database**.

On the **Import Data** dialog box, navigate to the Access database (this will usually be an ACCDB or MDB file). Select the file and click the **Import** button.

Excel displays the **Navigator** dialog box. The left pane of the dialog box has a list of tables and queries from the data source. On the right, there is a preview of the fields and values in the selected table.

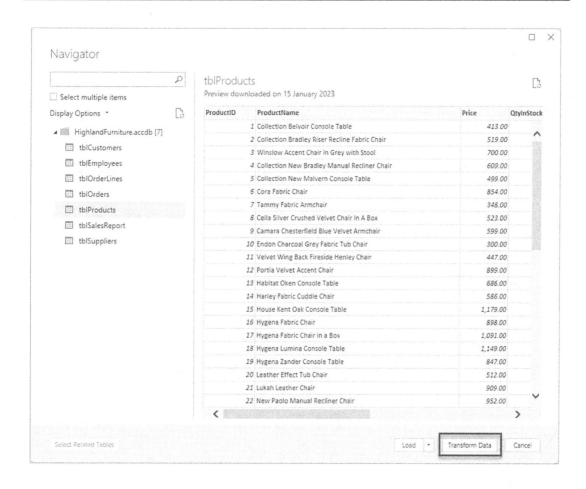

Select the source table and then click the **Transform Data** button to open the data as a new query in the Power Query Editor. The source table in this case is tblProducts.

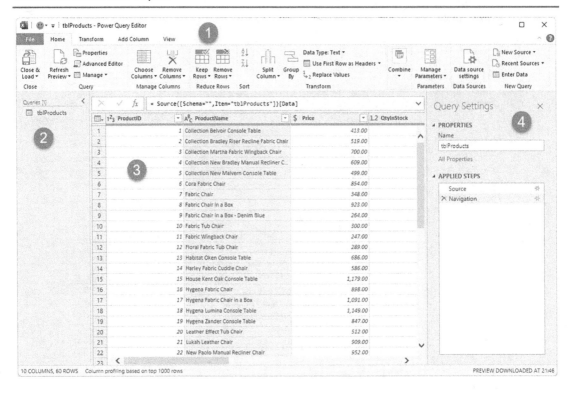

Below is a description of each part of the Power Query Editor user interface:

1. The ribbon has a File menu and four tabs: Home, Transform, Add Column, and View.

2. Use the Queries pane to locate data sources and tables.

3. The Data Preview displays the data, including any transformation performed on it.

4. The Query Settings pane has the query name under PROPERTIES, and APPLIED STEPS keeps a history of all the steps applied to the query.

Notice that the imported data has column headings with AutoFilter dropdown buttons. To remove a column from the query, select the column header (which selects the whole column) and click the **Remove Columns** button on the **Home** tab. We're removing the CategoryID, Notes, and SupplerID columns for our example.

To filter the dataset, click the AutoFilter button of the column you want to use to filter the data and deselect the values you don't want to include in the query. You can also clear the **Select All** checkbox and individually select the values you want to include in the query.

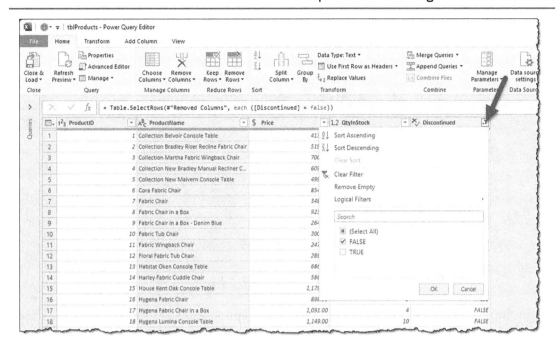

To apply a custom filter, select **Logical Filters** and follow the steps to enter your criteria. This option will differ depending on the data type of the field. For a text column, you'll get **Text Filters**. For a number column, you'll get **Number Filters,** etc.

When you have applied all the steps to transform the data as you would like to import it, you can now load the results to your Excel worksheet.

On the ribbon, select **Home** > **Close & Load** > **Close & Load To**.

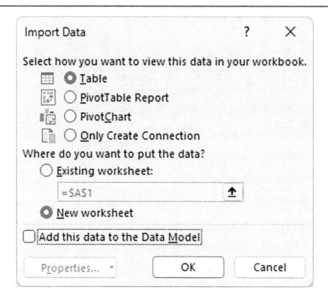

In the **Import Data** dialog box, accept the default settings of **Table** and **New Worksheet**, and then click **OK**.

That's it! Excel places the data in the new worksheet in your workbook named after the query. You can perform any formatting changes using Excel's formatting commands here.

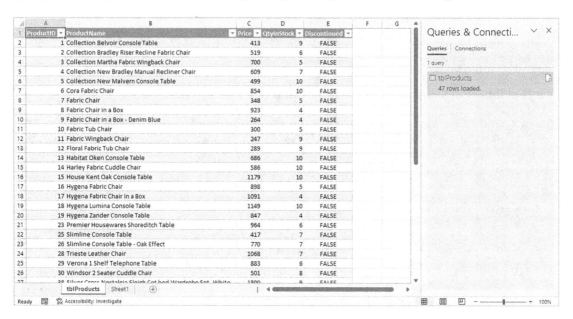

Modifying Your Query

Excel maintains a link to the original query for data generated using the Power Query Editor and displays this information in the **Queries and Connections** pane.

To edit the data using the Power Query Editor again, select any cell in the table in your worksheet, and click the **Edit** button in the **Edit** group on the **Query** tab. Note that the Query contextual tab is only available for data generated with a query and thus linked to a query in the Power Query Editor.

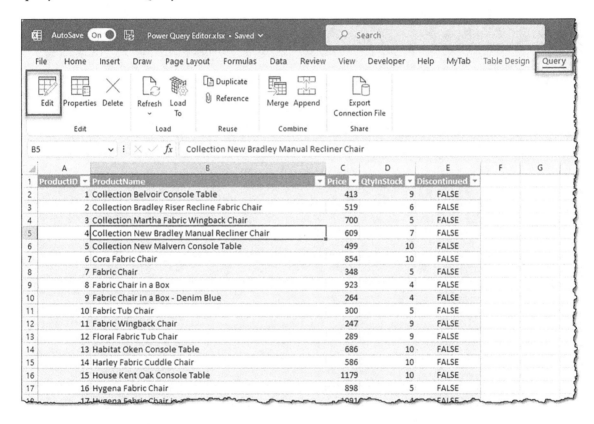

Excel opens the table in the Power Query Editor (see below), enabling you to further transform the data and load the results to your worksheet.

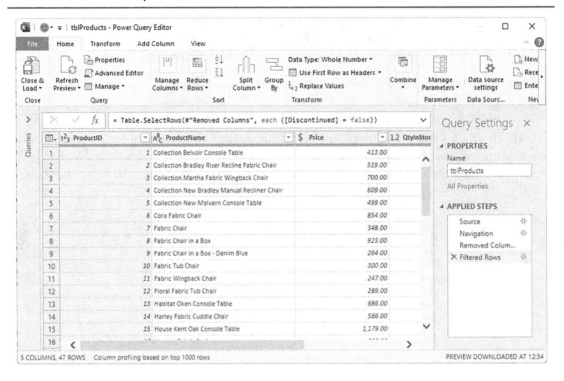

Chapter 4

Troubleshoot and Fix Formula Errors

In this chapter, we will cover how to:

- Use Trace commands to trace the precedents and dependents in your formulas to identify the relationships between the results and cell references.

- Step through a nested formula one level at a time to see results at each level.

- Use the Watch Window to display the value of a cell even when the cell is not in view.

Errors in simple Excel formulas are usually caused by syntax issues that are easily fixed by correcting the syntax. For example, Excel may generate an error because a formula is missing an opening or closing parenthesis. To fix the error, you simply add the parenthesis to the syntax. On the other hand, you may have a formula that doesn't generate an error, but it fails to return the expected result. This is called a logical error. These types of errors can be difficult to detect.

Programming tools tend to have debuggers that can be used to step through the code to identify and fix logical errors. Fortunately, Excel provides several tools that you can use to step through complex formulas to troubleshoot and fix logical errors.

Trace Precedents and Dependents

To help with troubleshooting your formula, you can use the **Trace Precedents** and **Trace Dependents** commands to show the relationships between the formula and any precedent or dependent cells using tracer arrows.

The Trace commands on the Excel ribbon are enabled by default (see image below). However, if they are disabled on your system, you need to enable them in Excel Options.

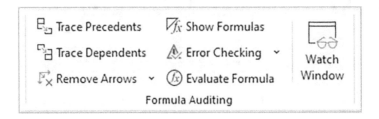

To enable Trace commands in **Excel Options**, do the following:

1. Select **File** > **Options** > **Advanced**.

2. Scroll down to the section labeled **Display options for this workbook** and select the workbook (if it is not already selected).

3. Select **All** under **For objects, show**.

Precedents are cells that are referred to by a formula in another cell. For example, if cell C2 contains the formula =A2+B2, then cells A2 and B2 are precedents to cell C2.

To Trace Precedents, do the following:

1. Select the cell that contains the formula that you want to trace.

2. On the **Formulas** tab, in the **Formula Auditing** group, click the **Trace Precedents** command button. Excel displays a tracer arrow to each cell or range that directly provides data to the active cell (cell with the formula).

Blue arrows will show cells without errors, while red arrows will show cells that cause errors. If the formula references a cell in another worksheet or workbook, a black arrow will point from the formula cell to a worksheet icon. If cells are referenced in other workbooks, they must be open before Excel can trace those dependencies.

3. If more levels of cells provide data to the formula, click Trace Precedents again.

Dependents are cells that contain formulas that refer to other cells. For example, if cell C2 contains the formula =A2+B2, then cell C2 is dependent on cells A2 and B2.

To Trace Dependents, follow these steps:

1. Select the cell that contains the formula for which you want to trace dependents.

2. On the **Formulas** tab, in the **Formula Auditing** group, click **Trace Dependents**. Excel displays a tracer arrow to each cell that is dependent on the active cell.

3. To identify further levels of dependent cells, click **Trace Dependents** again.

The tracer arrows in the example below show that cell B3 has several dependent cells with formulas in column C.

	A	B	C	D
1	Sales Tax Calculation			
2				
3	Tax Rate:	20%		
4				
5	Product	Price (excl. tax)	Tax	
6	Item 1	$40.00	$8.00	
7	Item 2	$58.00	$11.60	
8	Item 3	$85.00	$17.00	
9	Item 4	$47.00	$9.40	
10	Item 5	$56.00	$11.20	
11	Item 6	$28.00	$5.60	
12	Item 7	$31.00	$6.20	
13	Item 8	$65.00	$13.00	
14	Item 9	$25.90	$5.18	
15	Item 10	$78.30	$15.66	
16	Item 11	$69.30	$13.86	
17	Item 12	$56.80	$11.36	
18				

Removing Tracer Arrows

To remove all tracer arrows, on the **Formulas** tab, in the **Formula Auditing** group, click the arrow next to **Remove Arrows**.

To remove only the precedent or dependent arrows, click the down arrow next to **Remove Arrows** and select **Remove Precedent Arrows** or **Remove Dependent Arrows** from the drop-down list. If you have more than one level of tracer arrows, click the button again.

Evaluate a Formula

Sometimes formulas can be complex, for example, a nested formula with several nested levels. Knowing how the formula arrives at the final result may become difficult if there are several intermediate calculations and logical tests. Formulas that fail to produce the desired result may include logical errors that are difficult to spot at first glance.

The good news is that Excel has a tool called **Evaluate Formula**, which allows you to step through a complex formula. You can see how each level of the formula is evaluated, what the logical tests are doing, and the result at each level. Hence, you can more easily identify and resolve any logical errors in the syntax.

Example

In the following example, we'll use Evaluate Formula to evaluate the following nested formula:

=IF(D2 >= 10000,IF(E2 >= 15,D2*0.2,D2*0.15),IF(E2 >= 15,D2*0.15,D2*0.1))

The formula calculates the following:

- If a sales rep generates $10,000 in sales AND 15 signups, they earn a 20% commission on their sales amount.

- If a sales rep generates either $10,000 in sales OR 15 signups, they earn a 15% commission on their sales amount.

- If a sales rep generates less than $10,000 in sales and less than 15 signups, they earn a 10% commission on their sales amount.

The data being evaluated is shown in the image below.

fx	=IF(D2 >= 10000,IF(E2 >= 15,D2*0.2,D2*0.15),IF(E2 >= 15,D2*0.15,D2*0.1))					
	C	D	E	F	G	H
	Sales rep	Sales	Signups	Commission		
	Gilbert Higgins	$12,500	20	$2,500		
	Clinton Bradley	$14,300	25	$2,860		
	Bob Nash	$9,000	10	$900		
	Lee Powers	$8,050	5	$805		
	Mae Stevens	$5,000	7	$500		
	Inez Griffith	$8,900	10	$890		
	Theresa Hawkins	$7,900	10	$790		
	Felix Jacobs	$6,000	17	$900		
	Erik Lane	$11,000	18	$2,200		
	Jesse Garza	$12,676	12	$1,901		
	Alberta Fletcher	$13,163	14	$1,975		
	Melody Mendoza	$8,795	20	$1,319		
	Abraham Graves	$12,875	26	$2,575		
	Van Sims	$6,646	16	$997		

Follow the steps below to evaluate a formula:

1. Select the cell that you want to evaluate. In our example, it would be cell **F2**. Note that Excel can only evaluate one cell at a time.

2. On the **Formulas** tab, in the **Formula Auditing** group, click the **Evaluate Formula** button.

   Excel opens the **Evaluate Formula** dialog box. In the **Evaluation** box, Excel displays the evaluated formula and underlines the next statement to be evaluated.

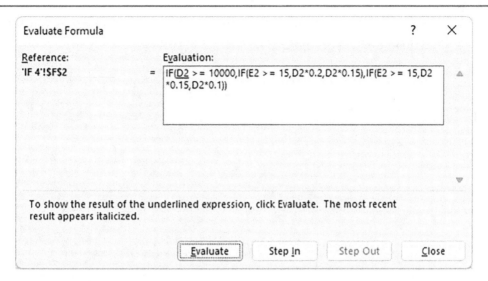

3. Click **Evaluate**. Excel evaluates the underlined statement and shows the result in italics. The next item to be evaluated is then underlined.

=IF(*12500* >= 1000,IF(E2 >= 15,D2*0.2,D2*0.15),IF(E2 >= 15,D2*0.15,D2*0.1))

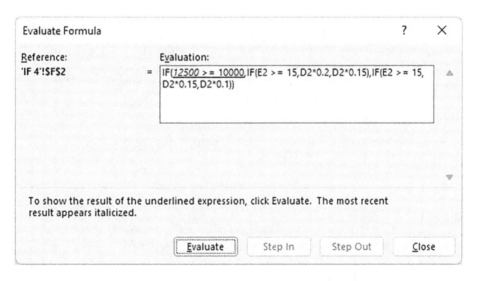

4. Click **Evaluate** again to evaluate the underlined statement. Excel shows the result in italics and underlines the next item to be evaluated.

=IF(*TRUE*,IF(E2 >= 15,D2*0.2,D2*0.15),IF(E2 >= 15,D2*0.15,D2*0.1))

In this case, the result of the test is TRUE. Hence, Excel will process elements of the first nested IF statement.

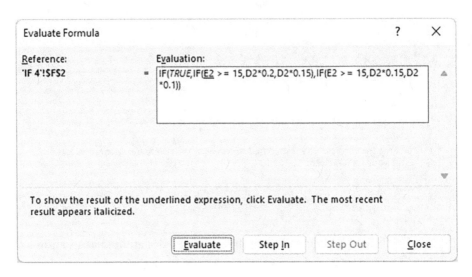

5. Click **Evaluate** to step through the formula and view the results until the final value is displayed in the **Evaluation** box.

   The process of stepping through the formula like this should help you to identify any logical errors in your formula. Pay attention to each element being evaluated, and the result returned.

6. Click **Restart** if you want to step through the formula again.

7. Click **Close** to dismiss the Evaluate Formula dialog box.

Note Some functions are recalculated each time the worksheet changes. Hence the Evaluate Formula tool could give results that are different from what appears in the cell if those functions are part of your formula. The following functions may not work well with Evaluate Formula: RAND, OFFSET, CELL, INDIRECT, NOW, TODAY, RANDBETWEEN, RANDARRAY, INFO, SUMIF (in some scenarios).

Using the Watch Window

Another way to troubleshoot logical errors in formulas is to use the **Watch Window** in Excel. You can use the Watch Window to inspect formula calculations and results in large worksheets. With the Watch Window, you don't need to scroll continually or go to different parts of your worksheet to see different results.

The Watch Window toolbar can be moved or docked like other toolbars in Excel. For example, you can move it and dock it at the bottom of the window. To undock the Watch Window toolbar, click its title bar and drag it from the docking position.

The Watch Window keeps track of the following properties of a cell: workbook, worksheet, name, cell reference, cell value, and the formula in a cell. You can only have one watch entry per cell. You can change data on the worksheet and view the Watch Window for how the change affects other cells with formulas.

The following example uses the Watch Window to monitor the value in cell B11 in our worksheet.

B11				fx	=IF(AVERAGE(A2:A9)>50,SUM(B2:B9),0)
	A	B	C	D	E	F	G
1	AVG	SUM					
2	45	47					
3	74	30					
4	26	40					
5	39	30					
6	90	77					
7	72	79					
8	28	48					
9	68	29					
10							
11	Result	380	Result if the average of A1:A8 is greater than 50				
12							

Follow the steps below to add a Watch item to the Watch Window:

1. Select the cells that you want to watch.

    To select all cells with formulas on your worksheet, select **Home** > **Editing** group > **Find & Replace** > **Go To Special** > **Formulas** > **OK**.

2. On the **Formulas** tab, in the **Formula Auditing** group, click the **Watch Window** button to display the Watch Window toolbar.

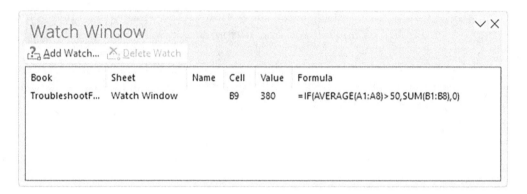

3. Click **Add Watch**.

4. Click **Add** in the **Add Watch** dialog. Here you can select a cell to watch (if it differs from the one selected in step 1).

5. Move the Watch Window toolbar and dock it to the bottom, left, or right side of the Excel window. To change the width of a column, for example, the **Book** column, drag the boundary on the right side of the column heading.

6. To display the cell for an entry in the Watch Window, double-click the entry to select the cell on the worksheet. Note that cells with references to other workbooks are only displayed in the Watch Window when the referenced workbook is open.

7. To close the Watch Window toolbar, on the **Formulas** tab, in the **Formula Auditing** group, click the **Watch Window** button to toggle it off.

Removing cells from the Watch Window

1. If the Watch Window toolbar is not open, click the **Watch Window** command button on the **Formulas** tab to display it.

2. Select the entry you want to remove. To select multiple entries, hold down the Ctrl key while clicking the entries.

3. Click **Delete Watch**.

4. To close the Watch Window toolbar, on the **Formulas** tab, in the **Formula Auditing** group, click the **Watch Window** button to toggle it off.

Chapter 5

Creating Advanced Formulas with Functions

This chapter covers the following:

- Creating conditional formulas with advanced IF functions.
- Generating random numbers, especially for producing test or sample data.
- Round up numbers to various decimal places.
- Manipulating and rearranging text strings with new Excel functions.
- Performing financial calculations with financial formulas.
- Installing the Analysis ToolPak for more specialized statistical and engineering functions.

My *Excel 2022 Basics* book covered the most commonly used Excel functions like IF, VLOOKUP, XLOOKUP, SUM, and COUNT. For brevity, this book focuses on more advanced functions not covered in that book. Functions are predesigned formulas, so they are tried and tested, and all you have to do is supply the inputs to get the results you need.

Creating Conditional Formulas with Advanced IF Functions

In addition to the basic IF function, Excel has several conditional functions that you can use to aggregate data based on certain conditions. There are functions like IFS, SUMIF, SUMIFS, COUNTIF, AVERAGEIF, etc., also referred to as advanced IF functions, which we'll cover in this section. For example, the IFS function can be used in place of convoluted nested IF statements. Several conditional aggregate functions enable you to use one function instead of two or more.

IFS Function

The IFS function enables you to carry out multiple logical tests and execute a statement corresponding to the first test that evaluates to TRUE. The tests need to be entered in the order you want the statements executed so that the right result is returned as soon as a test is passed. IFS was created as a better approach to nested IF statements, which can quickly become too complex.

Syntax

=IFS(logical_test1, value_if_true1, [logical_test2, value_if_true2], [logical_test3, value_if_true3],…)

Arguments

Argument	Description
logical_test1	Required. The condition that is being tested. It can evaluate to TRUE or FALSE.

value_if_true1	Required. The value returned if logical_test1 evaluates to TRUE.
logical_test2... logical_test127	Optional. An expression that evaluates to TRUE or FALSE. You can have up to 127 tests.
value_if_true2... value_if_true127	Optional. The value returned if a corresponding logical test evaluates to TRUE. You can have up to 127 values.

Remarks

The IFS function allows you to test up to 127 different tests. However, it is generally advised not to use too many tests with IF or IFS statements. Multiple tests need to be entered in the right order, and it can become too complex to update or maintain.

Tip As much as possible, use IFS instead of multiple nested IF statements. It is much easier to read when you have multiple conditions.

Example 1

In the example below, we use the IFS function to solve a problem we addressed earlier with nested IF statements. Notice how we don't need a nested function to achieve the same result.

In this problem, we want to assign grades to different ranges of exam scores.

Score and Grades
- 70 or above = MERIT
- 50 to 69 = CREDIT
- 40 to 49 = PASS
- less than 40 = FAIL

The following formula provides an ideal solution:

=IFS(B2>=70,"MERIT",B2>=50,"CREDIT", B2>=40,"PASS", B2<40,"FAIL")

	A	B	C	D	E	F	G	H	I	J
C2			fx	=IFS(B2>=70,"MERIT",B2>=50,"CREDIT", B2>=40,"PASS", B2<40,"FAIL")					

	A	B	C	D	E	F	G	H	I	J
1	Student	Mark	Grade							
2	Bruce	67	CREDIT							
3	Louis	57	CREDIT							
4	Earl	51	CREDIT							
5	Sean	74	MERIT							
6	Benjamin	50	CREDIT							
7	Joe	30	FAIL							
8	Shawn	95	MERIT							
9	Kenneth	8	FAIL							
10	Cynthia	30	FAIL							
11	Susan	57	CREDIT							
12	John	67	CREDIT							
13	Bruce	81	MERIT							
14	Louis	50	CREDIT							
15	Earl	30	FAIL							
16	Kenneth	79	MERIT							
17										

Formula explanation

=IFS(B2>=70,"MERIT",B2>=50,"CREDIT", B2>=40,"PASS", B2<40,"FAIL")

The IFS formula above has four logical tests in sequential order:

1. B2>=70,"MERIT"
2. B2>=50,"CREDIT"
3. B2>=40,"PASS"
4. B2<40,"FAIL"

B2 is a reference to the score. Each score is tested against each condition in sequential order. When a test returns TRUE, the corresponding grade is returned, and no further tests are carried out.

Example 2

In this example, we want to set different priority levels for re-ordering items depending on the number of items in stock.

Priority Level:
1. 5 or less = 1
2. 10 or less = 2
3. Less than 20 = 3

The formula we use to accomplish this task is:

=IFS(B2>20,"N/A",B2<=5,1, B2<=10,2, B2<20,3)

C2			✓ : ✕ ✓ fx	=IFS(B2>20,"N/A",B2<=5,1, B2<=10,2, B2<20,3)		
	A		B	C	D	E
1	**Product**		**# In stock**	**Reorder Priority**		
2	Cora Fabric Chair		10	2		
3	Tessa Fabric Chair		25	N/A		
4	Fabric Chair in a Box		9	2		
5	Lukah Leather Chair		10	2		
6	Fabric Tub Chair		4	1		
7	Fabric Wingback Chair		10	2		
8	Floral Fabric Tub Chair		15	3		
9	Habitat Oken Console Table		10	2		
10	Harley Fabric Cuddle Chair		10	2		
11	Leather Effect Tub Chair		5	1		
12	Habitat Fabric Chair		10	2		
13	Hygena Fabric Chair in a Box		5	1		
14	Hygena Lumina Console Table		15	3		

Formula explanation

=IFS(B2>20,"N/A",B2<=5,1, B2<=10,2, B2<20,3)

First, the formula has a test to mark the Reorder Priority of products greater than 20 as "N/A" (not applicable) as those have no re-order priority yet. Then several tests are defined in sequential order from the smallest value to the largest to ensure that the right corresponding value is returned as soon as a test is passed.

-🔅-**Tip** You can also apply **conditional formatting** to highlight the records with the highest priority. In this case, 1 is the highest priority. See my *Excel 2022 Basics* book for how to conditionally format a range.

SUMIF Function

The SUMIF function combines a math function and a logical function. It allows you to sum up data in a range based on the specified criteria.

Syntax

=SUMIF(range, criteria, [sum_range])

Arguments

Argument	Description
range	Required. The range you want to evaluate based on the condition in *criteria*.
criteria	Required. The condition (or logical test) that is used to determine which cells are summed up in range. This value can be an expression, cell reference, text, or function.

	Note: If this argument is text or includes logical or math symbols like greater than (>), it must be enclosed in double quotes (""). If this value is numeric, quotation marks are not required.
sum_range	Optional. Used to specify the sum range if it is different from the range specified in the range. If omitted, the range argument is used.

Remarks

- Cells in the range argument must be numbers, names (for example, named ranges or tables), arrays, or references that contain numbers. Text values and blanks are ignored.

- You can use wildcard characters (like a question mark "?" or an asterisk "*") as the criteria argument. A question mark matches any single character, while an asterisk matches any sequence of characters. Type a tilde (~) before the character to find an actual question mark or asterisk.

Example

The following example uses SUMIF to calculate the following:

- Total of all sales over $5,000.

- Total commissions paid out to salespeople who generated over $5,000 in sales.

We can achieve the desired results with two formulas:

=SUMIF(B2:B11,">5000")

=SUMIF(B2:B11,">5000", C2:C11)

| F2 | | | | f_x | =SUMIF(B2:B11,">5000") | |

	A	B	C	D	E	F	G
1	Salesperson	Sales	Commission		Sales over $5K		Formula text
2	Geraldine Simpson	$2,635	$132		Total	$59,250	=SUMIF(B2:B11,">5000")
3	Earnest Lambert	$7,227	$361		Total comm.	$2,963	=SUMIF(B2:B11,">5000", C2:C11)
4	Pauline Turner	$4,426	$221				
5	Miriam Abbott	$4,774	$239				
6	Willis Goodwin	$9,829	$491				
7	Claire Wilkerson	$20,000	$1,000				
8	Jamie Newman	$2,459	$123				
9	Andres Craig	$11,300	$565				
10	Dominic Gilbert	$2,566	$128				
11	Luz Fitzgerald	$10,894	$545				

Formula explanation

=SUMIF(B2:B11,">5000")

This formula uses the criteria argument of ">5000" to filter which values will be added to the sum from the range B2:B11.

=SUMIF(B2:B11,">5000", C2:C11)

Our second formula uses the criteria argument ">5000" to select the values in range B2:B11 (Sales) for which the corresponding values in range C2:C11 (Commission) will be added to the sum. So, even though we applied the criteria to B2:B11, the calculated values returned by the formula come from C2:C11.

SUMIFS Function

The SUMIFS function is like the SUMIF function, but you can use multiple criteria to determine which cells in a range are included in the sum. SUMIFS enables you to have up to 127 range/criteria pairs.

Syntax

=SUMIFS(sum_range, criteria_range1, criteria1, [criteria_range2, criteria2], ...)

Arguments

Argument	Description
sum_range	Required. The range of cells to sum up.
criteria_range1	Required. The range that is tested using Criteria1. Criteria_range1 and criteria1 are a pair where criteria1 is used to search criteria_range1 for matching values. Once items in the range are found, Excel sums up their corresponding values in sum_range.
criteria1	Required. The criteria used to filter criteria_range1 to select a subset of data. For example, criteria can be entered as 40, ">40", C6, "bolts", or "125".
criteria_range2, criteria2, ...	Optional. You can have additional range/criteria pairs up to 127.

Remarks

- If you are testing for text values, ensure the criteria are in quotation marks.

- You can use wildcard characters like the question mark (?) and asterisk (*) in your criteria to enable you to find matches that are not exact but similar. The question mark matches one character, and the asterisk matches a sequence of characters. To find a character like a question mark or asterisk, type a tilde sign (~) in front of the character.

- The criteria_range argument must reference a range with the same number of rows and columns as the sum_range argument.

Example

The following example sums up sales data using two criteria:

1. State name.

2. Items with 40 or more Orders (>=40).

The following formula achieves the result:

=SUMIFS($D$2:$D$12,$B$2:$B$12,F2,$C$2:$C$12,G2)

	A	B	C	D	E	F	G	H
	H2			fx =SUMIFS($D$2:$D$12,$B$2:$B$12,F2,$C$2:$C$12,G2)				
1	Name	States	No. Orders	Sales		States	Orders	Total Sales for matching orders
2	Bruce	New York	51	$74,298		New York	>=40	$140,407
3	Louis	New York	39	$46,039		Texas	>=40	$44,390
4	Earl	Washington	60	$65,252		California	>=40	$42,484
5	Sean	Washington	100	$61,847		Washington	>=40	$127,099
6	Benjamin	Texas	28	$33,340				
7	Joe	California	31	$95,778				
8	Shawn	Texas	35	$58,808				
9	Kenneth	California	39	$52,593				
10	Cynthia	California	51	$42,484				
11	Susan	Texas	80	$44,390				
12	Dav	New York	70	$66,109				
13								

Formula explanation

=SUMIFS($D$2:$D$12,$B$2:$B$12,F2,$C$2:$C$12,G2)

- The sum_range argument references the Sales column **D2:D12** (an absolute reference has been used - **$D$2:$D$12**).

- The criteria_range1 is **B2:B12** (an absolute reference has also been used here - **$B$2:$B$12**).

- Press F4, with the argument selected, to make this an absolute reference.

- The criteria1 argument is **F2**, which is a reference to the states we want to use as our criteria. Using a cell reference makes it easier to change this value. This argument has a relative reference because we want the cell reference to change as we copy the formula to other cells.

- The criteria_range2 is **$C$2:$C$12** (in absolute reference form).

- The criteria2 argument is **G2** (>=40). A cell reference has been used for this argument to make it easier to change.

We enter the formula in cell **H2** and then copy it down the column to calculate the **Total Sales** for orders that match the criteria for each state.

Tip To convert a relative reference to an absolute reference, manually add the dollar signs in the formula bar or select the reference in the formula (i.e., D2:D12) and press the **F4** key. Making the references absolute ensures they don't change when the formula is copied to other cells.

Using Named Ranges

One way to make a formula with absolute references easier to read is to use named ranges. Name ranges are absolute references by default and provide a cleaner look to your formula.

For example:
- Sales = D2:D12

- States = B2:B12
- Orders = C2:C12

With the named ranges in place, the formula looks like this:

=SUMIFS(Sales,States,F2,Orders,G2)

Instead of this:

=SUMIFS($D$2:$D$12,$B$2:$B$12,F2,$C$2:$C$12,G2)

IF			∨ : ✕ ✓ *fx*	=SUMIFS(Sales,States,F2,Orders,G2)		
	A	B	C	SUMIFS(sum_range, criteria_range1, criteria1, [criteria_range2, c...		
1	Name	States	No. Orders Sales	States	Orders	Total Sales for matching orders
2	Bruce	New York	51 $74,298	New York	>=40	Orders,G2)
3	Louis	New York	39 $46,039	Texas	>=40	$44,390
4	Earl	Washington	60 $65,252	California	>=40	$42,484
5	Sean	Washington	100 $61,847	Washington	>=40	$127,099
6	Benjamin	Texas	28 $33,340			
7	Joe	California	31 $95,778			
8	Shawn	Texas	35 $58,808			
9	Kenneth	California	39 $52,593			
10	Cynthia	California	51 $42,484			
11	Susan	Texas	80 $44,390			
12	Dav	New York	70 $66,109			
13						

COUNTIF Function

The COUNTIF function is a combination of a statistical function and a logical function. It allows you to count the number of cells that meet a criterion. For example, you can count only the values in a list of orders that exceed $1,000.

Syntax

=COUNTIF(range, criteria)

Arguments

Argument	Description
range	Required. The group of cells that you want to count. This argument can contain numbers, a named range, or references that contain numbers.
criteria	Required. The condition used to determine which cells will be counted. This argument can be a cell reference, text, expression, or function. For example, you can use a number like 40, a logical comparison like ">=40", a cell reference like D10, or a word like "bolts."

Remarks

- If the criteria argument is a text value or includes logical or math symbols, like greater than (>), it must be enclosed in double quotes ("").
- If criteria is a numeric value, quotation marks are not required.

Example

In this example, we're using COUNTIF to count all Sales over $5,000.

The formula we use is:

=COUNTIF(B2:B11,">5000")

C14		f_x	=COUNTIF(B2:B11,">5000")

	A	B	C	D
1	**Salesperson**	**Sales**	**Commission**	**Formula text**
2	Bruce	$2,635	$132	
3	Louis	$7,227	$361	
4	Earl	$4,426	$221	
5	Sean	$4,774	$239	
6	Benjamin	$9,829	$491	
7	Joe	$20,000	$1,000	
8	Shawn	$2,459	$123	
9	Kenneth	$11,300	$565	
10	Cynthia	$2,566	$128	
11	Susan	$10,894	$545	
12				
13	**Report**			
14	**Count of sales over $5,000**		5	=COUNTIF(B2:B11,">5000")
15	**Count of commissions over $200**		7	=COUNTIF(C2:C11,">200")
16				

The first argument is the range we want to count - **B2:B11**.

The second argument is the criteria - greater than $5,000 ("">5000"").

Note that the criteria argument is enclosed in quotes because it includes a comparison operator.

Other examples

In the following examples, we have a list of orders that we query with different COUNTIF formulas in a report. The results and formulas are shown in the image below.

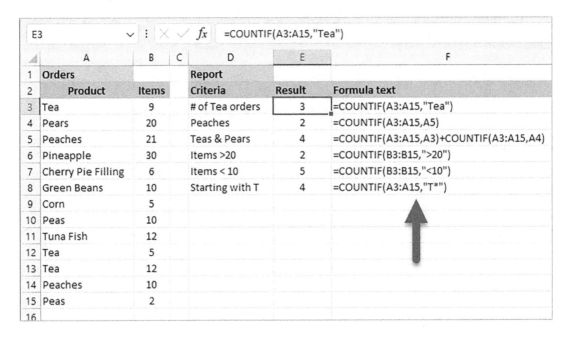

COUNTIFS Function

The COUNTIFS function enables you to count values in multiple ranges using multiple criteria to determine the values to count.

Syntax

=COUNTIFS(criteria_range1, criteria1, [criteria_range2, criteria2]…)

Arguments

Argument	Description
criteria_range1	Required. The first range you want to evaluate using the associated criteria, which is criteria1.
criteria1	Required. The first criteria argument, which pairs with criteria_range1. It could be a number, cell reference, expression, or text that defines which cells will be counted. For example, criteria can be expressed as 40, ">=40", D10, "bolts", or "40".
criteria_range2, criteria2, ...	Optional. Additional ranges and criteria pairs. You can have a total of 127 range/criteria pairs.

Remarks

- Each additional range must have the same number of rows and columns as criteria_range1. The ranges do not have to be adjacent to each other.

- If the criteria argument points to an empty cell, the COUNTIFS function treats the empty cell as a 0 value.

- If you are testing for text values, for example, "apples," make sure the criterion is in quotation marks.

- You can use wildcard characters like the question mark (?) and asterisk (*) in your criteria to enable you to find matches that are similar but not the same. The question mark matches any character, and the asterisk matches a sequence of characters. To find a character like a question mark or asterisk, type a tilde sign (~) in front of the character.

91

Example

The following example counts the number of people for each State with 40 or more Orders. This problem requires using two criteria to evaluate two columns. We will use the state name and ">=40" to filter the rows to be counted.

We apply the following formula to solve the problem:

=COUNTIFS(State,F2,Orders,G2)

Range names:
- State = B2:B12
- Orders = C2:C12

	A	B	C	D	E	F	G	H	I
1	Name	State	Orders	Sales		States	Orders	# People	Formula text
2	Bruce	New York	51	$74,298		New York	>=40	2	=COUNTIFS(State,F2,Orders,G2)
3	Louis	New York	39	$46,039		Texas	>=40	1	=COUNTIFS(State,F3,Orders,G3)
4	Earl	Washington	60	$65,252		California	>=40	1	=COUNTIFS(State,F4,Orders,G4)
5	Sean	Washington	100	$61,847		Washington	>=40	2	=COUNTIFS(State,F5,Orders,G5)
6	Benjamin	Texas	28	$33,340					
7	Joe	California	31	$95,778					
8	Shawn	Texas	35	$58,808					
9	Kenneth	California	39	$52,593					
10	Cynthia	California	51	$42,484		State = B2:B12			
11	Susan	Texas	80	$44,390		Orders = C2:12			
12	Dav	New York	70	$66,109					
13									

Formula explanation:

=COUNTIFS(State,F2,Orders,G2)

- The criteria_range1 argument references the range B2:B12 for which the range name **State** has been used.

- The criteria1 argument is cell **F2**, which has the State we want to use as our criteria. Using a cell reference here makes it easier to change the value.

  This argument is a relative cell reference because we want it to change (relatively) as we copy the formula to other cells.

- The criteria_range2 is the range C2:C12, which has the range name **Orders** in the worksheet. We will be using criteria2 to evaluate this range.

- The criteria2 argument is **G2**, which is the expression **>=40**. A cell reference is used for this argument to make it easier to change the criteria.

We enter the formula in cell **H2** and copy it down the column to count the number of people with orders that match the criteria for each state.

AVERAGEIF Function

The AVERAGEIF function is a combination of a statistical function and a logical function. AVERAGEIF returns the average (or arithmetic mean) of all the cells in a range that meet a specified condition.

Syntax

=AVERAGEIF(range, criteria, [average_range])

Arguments

Argument	Description
range	Required. A reference to one or more cells to average. This argument can include numbers, cell references, or named ranges.
criteria	Required. An expression that determines which cells are included in the average.
average_range	Optional. The actual set of cells to average, if not the cells in the *range* argument. If this argument is omitted, *range* is used.

Remarks

- AVERAGEIF will return the error #DIV/0! if no cells in *range* meet the criteria.

93

- AVERAGEIF will return the error #DIV/0! if *range* is a blank or text string.

- If a cell in *criteria* is empty, it is treated as zero (0).

- Cells in the range argument that contain logical values like TRUE or FALSE are ignored.

- You can use wildcard characters like the question mark (?) and asterisk (*) in your criteria to find matches that are similar but not the same. A question mark matches any single character, while an asterisk matches a sequence of characters. To find a character like a question mark or asterisk, type a tilde sign (~) in front of the character.

- *Average_range* does not necessarily need to be the same number of rows and columns as *range*. The average is performed by using the top-left cell in average_range plus cells that match the same number of rows and columns in the range argument. See examples in the table below:

range	average_range	Cells evaluated and averaged
A1:A10	B1:B10	B1:B10
A1:A10	B1:B5	B1:B10
A1:B5	C1:C3	C1:D5

Example

In the following example, we use the AVERAGEIF function to calculate the average test scores for students per subject. We want to group the data by **Subject** (for example, Biology, Chemistry, Math, etc.) and average each group by **Score**.

The range used to filter the averaged data is B2:B16, and the range that averaged is C2:C16. The formula uses range names for the referenced ranges to make them absolute references.

| F2 | | | f_x | =AVERAGEIF(Subjects,E2,Scores) | | |

	A	B	C	D	E	F	G
1	**Student**	**Subject**	**Score**		**Subject**	**Average**	**Formula text**
2	Bruce	Math	75		Math	68.4	=AVERAGEIF(Subjects,E2,Scores)
3	Louis	Chemistry	61		Chemistry	53.8	=AVERAGEIF(Subjects,E3,Scores)
4	Earl	Biology	67		English	68.0	=AVERAGEIF(Subjects,E4,Scores)
5	Sean	English	74		Biology	69.7	=AVERAGEIF(Subjects,E5,Scores)
6	Benjamin	Math	86				
7	Joe	Chemistry	58				
8	Shawn	Biology	74				
9	Kenneth	English	70				
10	Cynthia	Math	55				
11	Susan	Chemistry	49				
12	John	Math	76		*Subjects = B2:B16*		
13	Bruce	English	60		*Scores = C2:C16*		
14	Louis	Biology	68				
15	Earl	Chemistry	47				
16	Kenneth	Math	50				
17							

Formula explanation:

=AVERAGEIF(Subjects,E2,Scores)

Subjects = B2:B16
Scores = C2:C16

- The range argument references cells B2:B16 (named Subjects), which is used to filter the values to be averaged.

- The criteria argument is **E2**, which is a reference to our criteria. Using a cell reference makes it easier to change the criteria on the worksheet. This argument is a relative reference because we want the criteria to change (relatively) as we copy the formula to other cells.

- The average_range argument references cells C2:C16 (named Scores), which is the range we want to average based on the criteria.

  We enter the formula in cell F2 to return the average for Math, then copy the formula to cells F3:F5 to display the average for the other subjects.

AVERAGEIFS Function

The AVERAGEIFS function returns the average (arithmetic mean) of all cells that meet a set of criteria. This function allows you to specify several criteria pairs to select the data to be included in the average. An IFS function enables you to create several range/criteria pairs to select the data that meet the criteria.

The function identifies items that meet the criteria in one column and averages corresponding items in another. You can have up to a maximum of 127 range/criteria pairs, as you can only have 255 arguments in an Excel function.

Syntax

=AVERAGEIFS(average_range, criteria_range1, criteria1, [criteria_range2, criteria2], ...)

Arguments

Argument	Description
average_range	Required. The range of cells for which you want the average calculated.
criteria_range1	Required. The range to evaluate using criteria1.
criteria1	Required. The criteria used to evaluate criteria1_range to select matching data. For example, criteria can be entered as 40, ">40", C6, "bolts", or "125".
Criteria_range2, criteria2, ...	Optional. You can have additional range/criteria pairs, up to 127 total pairs.

Example

This example shows a list of orders from different sales reps for several states. We want to find the average sales per state for entries with 10 or more orders (>=10).

We can use the following formula to achieve the result:

=AVERAGEIFS(Sales,States,F2,Orders,G2)

Sales = D2:D12
States = B2:B12
Orders = C2:C12

	H2				$f\!x$	=AVERAGEIFS(Sales,States,F2,Orders,G2)			
	A	B	C	D	E	F	G	H	I
1	Name	State	Orders	Sales		States	Orders	Avg Sales 10+ orders	Formula text
2	Bruce	New York	12	$74,298		New York	>=10	$70,204	=AVERAGEIFS(Sales,States,F2,Orders,G2)
3	Louis	New York	5	$46,039		Texas	>=10	$58,808	=AVERAGEIFS(Sales,States,F3,Orders,G3)
4	Earl	Washington	15	$65,252		California	>=10	$52,593	=AVERAGEIFS(Sales,States,F4,Orders,G4)
5	Sean	Washington	11	$61,847		Washington	>=10	$63,550	=AVERAGEIFS(Sales,States,F5,Orders,G5)
6	Benjamin	Texas	9	$33,340					
7	Joe	California	3	$30,000					
8	Shawn	Texas	20	$58,808		Sales = D2:D12			
9	Kenneth	California	12	$52,593		States = B2:B12			
10	Cynthia	California	8	$42,484		Orders = C2:C12			
11	Susan	Texas	2	$20,000					
12	Dav	New York	10	$66,109					
13									
14									
15	The average sales per state for entries with 10 or more orders.								
16									
17									

Formula explanation:

=AVERAGEIFS(Sales,States,F2,Orders,G2)

- The average_range argument references D2:D12 (named Sales), the range for which we calculate the average.

- The criteria_range1 is B2:B12 for which a range name States has been used.

- The criteria1 argument is F2, a cell reference to the value used as the criteria. A cell reference makes it easier to change the criteria on the worksheet.

  This argument is a relative reference as we want it to change as we copy the formula to other cells.

- The criteria_range2 argument is C2:C12 (named Orders) has been used.

- The criteria2 argument is cell G2, which references our criteria (>=10). This argument is a matching pair for criteria_range2. A cell reference has been used to make it easier to change the criteria if needed.

The first criteria_range/criteria pair filters the data by State, and the second criteria_range/criteria pair filters the data by Orders. The formula then returns the average of the filtered data.

The formula is entered in cell H2 and copied to H3:H5 to calculate the average for the other states.

MAXIFS and MINIFS Functions

The MAXIFS and MINIFS functions are an extension of the MAX and MIN functions to include a conditional component in their functionality. MAXIFS returns the maximum value of all cells that meet the specified criteria. MINIFS returns the minimum value of all cells that meet the specified criteria. You can specify more than one set of criteria to determine which data is selected to be part of the evaluation.

An IFS function enables you to create several range/criteria pairs to narrow down the data to only those that meet the criteria. The functions identify items that meet the criteria in one column and calculate corresponding items in another.

You can have up to a maximum of 127 range/criteria pairs, as you can only have 255 arguments in an Excel function.

Syntax

=MAXIFS(max_range, criteria_range1, criteria1, [criteria_range2, criteria2], ...)

=MINIFS(min_range, criteria_range1, criteria1, [criteria_range2, criteria2], ...)

Arguments – similar for both functions

Argument	Description
max_range (MAX function) min_range(MIN function)	Required. The actual range of cells for which we want the maximum or minimum value determined.
criteria_range1	Required. The range evaluated using criteria1.
criteria1	Required. The criteria used to determine which cells in criteria_range1 will be part of the calculation. This argument can be a number, expression, or text. For example, criteria can be entered as 40, ">40", C6, "bolts", or "125".
criteria_range2, criteria2, ...	Optional. You can have additional range/criteria pairs, up to 127 total pairs.

Remarks

- The max_range (or min_range) and criteria_range arguments must have the same number of rows and columns. Otherwise, these functions return the #VALUE! error.

- The range we use to filter the data does not necessarily have to be the same range from which we want to generate the max or min value.

Example

In this example, we want to produce reports that show the minimum and maximums sales per state. However, we only want to evaluate entries with 10 or more orders (>=10). So, we have different criteria that we want to use to determine the data to be evaluated.

Formulas

The following formulas return the desired results.

Maximum:
=MAXIFS(Sales,States,F3,Orders,G3)

Minimum:
=MINIFS(Sales,States,F10,Orders,G10)

	A	B	C	D	E	F	G	H	I
1	**Name**	**State**	**Orders**	**Sales**		**Max Sales**			
2	Bruce	New York	12	$74,298		**States**	**Orders**	**Max Sales**	**Formula Text**
3	Louis	New York	5	$46,039		New York	>=10	$74,298	=MAXIFS(Sales,States,F3,Orders,G3)
4	Earl	Washington	15	$65,252		Texas	>=10	$58,808	=MAXIFS(Sales,States,F4,Orders,G4)
5	Sean	Washington	11	$61,847		California	>=10	$52,593	=MAXIFS(Sales,States,F5,Orders,G5)
6	Benjamin	Texas	10	$33,340		Washington	>=10	$65,252	=MAXIFS(Sales,States,F6,Orders,G6)
7	Joe	California	3	$30,000					
8	Shawn	Texas	20	$58,808		**Min Sales**			
9	Kenneth	California	12	$52,593		**States**	**Orders**	**Min sales**	**Formula Text**
10	Cynthia	California	8	$42,484		New York	>=10	$66,109	=MINIFS(Sales,States,F10,Orders,G10)
11	Susan	Texas	2	$20,000		Texas	>=10	$33,340	=MINIFS(Sales,States,F11,Orders,G11)
12	Dav	New York	10	$66,109		California	>=10	$52,593	=MINIFS(Sales,States,F12,Orders,G12)
13						Washington	>=10	$61,847	=MINIFS(Sales,States,F13,Orders,G13)
14									

Formula explanation

Both functions use identical cell references and criteria arguments. So, they can be described together.

=MAXIFS(Sales,States,F3,Orders,G3)

=MINIFS(Sales,States,F10,Orders,G10)

- The first argument references D2:D12, which has the range name **Sales**. We want to evaluate this range for the maximum and minimum values.

- The criteria_range1 argument is referencing B2:B12 (named **States**). This argument makes up the first range/criteria pair we're using to filter the data to be evaluated.

- The criteria1 argument is **F2**, a cell reference to the criteria - **New York**. Using a cell reference makes it easier to change the criteria.

- The criteria_range2 argument is C2:C12 (named **Orders**). Criteria_range2 is part of the second range/criteria pair.

- The criteria2 argument is cell **G2** which holds the criteria for the number of orders, ">=10". Criteria2 is part of the second range/criteria pair used to filter the data to be evaluated. A cell reference has been used to make it easier to change the criteria.

To display the results, we enter the MAXIFS formula in cell H3 and copy it to the other cells for which we want to display maximum sales. For the minimum values, the MINIFS formula is entered in cell H10 and copied to the other cells displaying the minimum sales.

IFERROR Function

You can use IFERROR to trap errors in Excel formulas and return a custom message. This function provides a more user-friendly experience, especially if you're developing a worksheet for end-users and anticipate errors in certain data cells. Otherwise, you often do need to see the errors Excel generates so you can fix them.

This method is similar to how errors are trapped and handled in computer code. IFERROR can trap the following error types: #VALUE!, #N/A, #DIV/0!, #REF!, #NAME?, #NUM!, or #NULL!.

Syntax

=IFERROR(value, value_if_error)

Arguments

Argument	Description
value	Required. A cell reference or formula that's checked for an error.
value_if_error	Required. The value to be returned if the formula identifies an error.

Remarks

- If either *value* or *value_if_error* points to an empty cell, IFERROR treats it as an empty string value ("").

- If *value* is an array formula, IFERROR returns an array, one for each cell in the results range.

101

Example

In the following example, we use the IFERROR formula to trap any errors in our formula in column C and return a text message **Entry error**.

The FORMULATEXT function used in D2:D9 reveals the formulas in C2:C9.

C2		∨ : ✕ ✓ fx	=IFERROR(B2/A2,"Entry error")	
	A	B	C	D
1	**Target**	**Actual sold**	**Percentage**	**Formula text**
2	200	35	18%	=IFERROR(B2/A2,"Entry error")
3	10	0	0%	=IFERROR(B3/A3,"Entry error")
4	120	50	42%	=IFERROR(B4/A4,"Entry error")
5	300	5	2%	=IFERROR(B5/A5,"Entry error")
6	0	60	Entry error	=IFERROR(B6/A6,"Entry error")
7	50	0	0%	=IFERROR(B7/A7,"Entry error")
8		10	Entry error	=IFERROR(B8/A8,"Entry error")
9	250	120	48%	=IFERROR(B9/A9,"Entry error")
10				

IFNA Function

The IFNA function is for handling #N/A errors. Excel displays the #NA error when a value is unavailable to a formula or function. Use IFNA when you want to trap and handle only #N/A errors.

You're more likely to encounter #N/A errors with lookup and reference functions when a value referenced in the formula is not in the source. You usually want to display other errors as they may reveal bugs in your formula that need fixing.

IFNA returns the value you specify if your formula encounters the #N/A error. Otherwise, it returns the result of the formula.

Syntax:

= IFNA(value, value_if_na)

Arguments

Argument	Description
value	Required. The expression that is checked for an error. It can be a value, cell reference, or formula. When using IFNA with VLOOKUP, the VLOOKUP formula will be this argument.
value_if_na	Required. The value the formula returns when it encounters a #N/A error.

Example

The following example uses the IFNA function to handle a #N/A error generated when the VLOOKUP function cannot find the provided lookup_value in the table_array.

The formula in E2, without IFNA, returns #N/A. Conversely, the formula in E3 traps the error with IFNA and provides a more user-friendly message.

=IFNA(VLOOKUP(D3,A3:B11,2,FALSE),"Not found")

| E3 | | | f_x | =IFNA(VLOOKUP(D3,A3:B11,2,FALSE),"Not found") |

	A	B	C	D	E	F
1	**Product**	**Cost**		**Product**	**Cost**	**Formula text**
2	Beer	$1.50		Walnuts	#N/A	=VLOOKUP(D2,A2:B10,2,FALSE)
3	Brownie Mix	$4.20		Walnuts	Not found	=IFNA(VLOOKUP(D3,A3:B11,2,FALSE),"Not found")
4	Cake Mix	$4.80				
5	Chai	$1.80				
6	Chocolate Biscuits Mix	$5.20				
7	Coffee	$2.00				
8	Green Tea	$2.00				
9	Scones	$4.90				
10	Tea	$1.30				
11						

Math Functions

The mathematics functions in Excel can be found by clicking the Math & Trig command button on the Formulas tab of the ribbon. The dropdown menu lists all the Math & Trig functions. This category of functions in Excel ranges from common arithmetic functions to complex functions used by mathematicians and engineers.

Our focus here will be on the arithmetic functions, as many Excel trigonometric functions apply to math problems requiring specialist knowledge outside the scope of this book.

RANDBETWEEN Function

The RANDBETWEEN function returns a random integer between two numbers you specify. This function comes in handy whenever you need to generate sample data between two numbers. For example, if you want to generate sample data between 1 and 100 in several cells, you could use RANDBETWEEN to generate a random number in one cell and copy the formula over the required range.

Syntax

=RANDBETWEEN(bottom, top)

Arguments

Argument	Description
Bottom	Required. The smallest integer to be returned.
Top	Required. The largest integer to be returned.

Random values from RANDBETWEEN are regenerated each time the worksheet is recalculated. If you don't want the values to change each time the worksheet is recalculated, copy them to the clipboard, then use **Paste Special** > **Values** to convert them to static values.

To generate a random number that doesn't change, enter the formula in the formula bar, press F9 to convert the formula to a static value, then press **Enter** to insert the value in the cell.

Example

The following example uses RANDBETWEEN to generate sample data for student scores between 0 and 100.

= RANDBETWEEN(0,100)

B4				fx	=RANDBETWEEN(0,100)
	A	B	C	D	E	F
1	Test Score Sample Data					
2						
3	Student	Score				
4	Bruce	70				
5	Louis	82				
6	Earl	28				
7	Sean	44				
8	Benjamin	3				
9	Joe	19				
10	Shawn	38				
11	Kenneth	34				
12	Cynthia	5				
13	Susan	7				

Tip To keep only the generated values without the formula, generate the sample data in a different part of your worksheet and copy and paste only the values into your target range. For example, if you wanted random values in cells B2:B10, generate the values using RANDBETWEEN in cells C2:C10 and then copy and paste only the values in B2:B10, then delete the values in C2:C10.

RANDARRAY Function

RANDARRAY is a dynamic array function that returns random numbers. An array can be seen as a row of values, a column of values, or a combination of both. This function is an improvement on RANDBETWEEN, which returns only one value and must be copied to the entire range for multiple random numbers. RANDARRAY can return multiple values with one formula for your specified range. You can also specify whether you want whole numbers or decimal values.

Note   This function is currently only available to Microsoft 365 subscribers.

Syntax

=RANDARRAY([rows],[columns],[min],[max],[whole_number])

Argument	Description
rows	Optional. The number of rows returned. If omitted, RANDARRAY will return a single row.
columns	Optional. The number of columns returned. If omitted, RANDARRAY will return a single column.
min	Optional. The minimum number to return.
max	Optional. The maximum number to return.
whole_number	Optional. Set this option to TRUE for whole numbers and FALSE for decimal values. If omitted, the default is FALSE, i.e., decimal values.

Remarks:

- If you omit both the rows and columns arguments, RANDARRAY returns a single value.

- If you omit the min and max arguments, RANDARRY returns numbers between 0 and 1.

- The max argument must be greater than the min argument. Otherwise, RANDARRAY returns a #VALUE! error.

Example

The following example generates sample numbers to be used as test data. The RANDARRAY formula is in cell B2, spilling the result over the range B2:E13. Note that we do not need to copy the formula to the other cells.

=RANDARRAY(12,4,500,1000,TRUE)

B2		fx	=RANDARRAY(12,4,500,1000,TRUE)			
	A	B	C	D	E	F	G
1		**2022**	**2023**	**2024**	**2025**		
2	Jan	$501.00	$817.00	$530.00	$711.00		
3	Feb	$959.00	$887.00	$710.00	$739.00		
4	Mar	$532.00	$794.00	$727.00	$894.00		
5	Apr	$668.00	$972.00	$759.00	$839.00		
6	May	$945.00	$683.00	$751.00	$698.00		
7	Jun	$978.00	$509.00	$561.00	$911.00		
8	Jul	$626.00	$669.00	$911.00	$915.00		
9	Aug	$662.00	$573.00	$849.00	$971.00		
10	Sep	$829.00	$699.00	$966.00	$962.00		
11	Oct	$822.00	$813.00	$719.00	$720.00		
12	Nov	$751.00	$823.00	$889.00	$998.00		
13	Dec	$692.00	$983.00	$878.00	$884.00		
14							

Formula explanation

=RANDARRAY(12,4,500,1000,TRUE)

The row and column numbers are 12 and 4. The min and max numbers are 500 and 1000. The whole_number argument is set to TRUE to return whole numbers. The range is formatted as Currency.

Note Random values from RANDARRAY are regenerated each time the worksheet is recalculated. If you don't want the values to change each time the worksheet is recalculated, copy them to the clipboard, then use **Paste Special > Values** to convert them to static values.

SEQUENCE Function

SEQUENCE is a dynamic array function that allows you to generate a list of sequential numbers in an array. You can also specify an interval. An array can be a row of values, a column of values, or a combination of both. You can manually generate a series of numbers in Excel using the AutoFill feature. SEQUENCE offers the function equivalent of creating a series.

Note This function is currently only available to Microsoft 365 subscribers.

Syntax

=SEQUENCE(rows,[columns],[start],[step])

Arguments

Argument	Description
rows	Required. The number of rows to create.
columns	Optional. The number of columns to create. The default is 1 if this argument is omitted.
start	Optional. The starting number. The default is 1 if this argument is omitted.
step	Optional. The increment applied to each subsequent value in the array. The default is 1 if this argument is omitted.

Remarks

The result from SEQUENCE will spill on the worksheet if it's the final result of a formula. Excel will create the right-sized range to display the result. You can also use SEQUENCE as an argument within another formula to generate an array of values.

Example 1

The following example uses SEQUENCE to generate even numbers in five columns and five rows.

=SEQUENCE(5,5,0,2)

The formula has 5 for both the rows and columns arguments. The start argument is 0, and the step is 2.

	A	B	C	D	E	F
1	0	2	4	6	8	
2	10	12	14	16	18	
3	20	22	24	26	28	
4	30	32	34	36	38	
5	40	42	44	46	48	
6						
7						

A1 — fx =SEQUENCE(5,5,0,2)

Example 2

Excel stores date values internally as serial numbers, so you can use SEQUENCE to generate dates with a specified interval. To display the result as a date, ensure the spill range is formatted as an Excel **Date**.

The following example generates the Monday date for 10 weeks from our specified starting date, 10/10/2022.

| B2 | | | ✓ : ✕ ✓ *fx* | =SEQUENCE(10,,DATEVALUE("10/10/2022"),7) | | | | |

◢	A	B	C	D	E	F	G	H
1	**Week starting Monday**							
2	Week 1	10/10/2022						
3	Week 2	17/10/2022						
4	Week 3	24/10/2022						
5	Week 4	31/10/2022						
6	Week 5	07/11/2022						
7	Week 6	14/11/2022						
8	Week 7	21/11/2022						
9	Week 8	28/11/2022						
10	Week 9	05/12/2022						
11	Week 10	12/12/2022						
12								

Formula explanation:

=SEQUENCE(10,,DATEVALUE("10/10/2022"),7)

The rows argument is 10 to specify the ten rows of dates we want to return. The columns argument has been omitted as we only want one column. For the starting date, the formula uses the DATEVALUE function to return the serial number for the provided date string. The step argument is 7, which increments each subsequent number by 7. Excel displays the serial numbers returned by DATEVALUE as dates because the spill range has the Date number format.

Note You might be thinking that it would just be easier to generate the list of dates on the worksheet by adding 7 to the second week and using autofill to populate the other cells. That's correct. The SEQUENCE function is more useful when you need to generate sequential values as an array argument within another formula.

ROUND Function

The ROUND function rounds a number to a specified number of digits. For example, if you have 25.4568 in cell A1 and you want to round the figure to two decimal places, you can use the following formula:

=ROUND(A1, 2)

The function will return: 25.46

Syntax

=ROUND(number, num_digits)

Arguments

Argument	Description
number	Required. This argument is the number that you want to round.
num_digits	Required. The number of decimal places to which you want to round the number.

Remarks

- The number is rounded to the specified number of decimal places if num_digits is greater than 0 (zero).
- The number is rounded to the nearest integer if num_digits is 0.
- The number is rounded to the left of the decimal point if num_digits is less than 0.
- Use the ROUNDUP function to always round up (away from zero).
- Use the ROUNDDOWN function to always round down (toward zero).

Examples

In the following examples, the ROUND function is applied to several values. The table displays the formula, the result, and a description of the outcome.

Formula	Result	Description
=ROUND(3.15, 1)	3.2	Rounds 3.15 to one decimal place.
=ROUND(4.149, 1)	4.1	Rounds 4.149 to one decimal place.
=ROUND(-2.475, 2)	-2.48	Rounds -2.475 to two decimal places.
=ROUND(57.5, -1)	60	Rounds 57.5 to one decimal place to the left of the decimal point.
=ROUND(671.3,-3)	1000	Rounds 671.3 to the nearest multiple of 1000.
=ROUND(1.78,-1)	0	Rounds 1.78 to the nearest multiple of 10.
=ROUND(-70.45,-2)	-100	Rounds -70.45 to the nearest multiple of 100.

ROUNDUP Function

The ROUNDUP function rounds a number up, away from 0 (zero).

Syntax

=ROUNDUP(number, num_digits)

Arguments

Argument	Description
number	Required. This argument is for the number that you want to round up.
num_digits	Required. The number of decimal places to which you want to round up the number.

Remarks

- ROUNDUP is like ROUND but always rounds a number up.

- Number is rounded up to the specified number of decimal places if num_digits is greater than 0 (zero).

- Number is rounded up to the nearest integer if num_digits is 0.

- Number is rounded up to the left of the decimal point if num_digits is less than 0.

Examples

In the following examples, ROUNDUP is applied to several values. The table displays the value, result, formula, and description.

	A	B	C	D
1	Value	Rounded up	Formula text	Description
2	3.15	3.2	=ROUNDUP(A2, 1)	Rounds 3.15 up to one decimal place.
3	4.149	5	=ROUNDUP(A3, 0)	Rounds 4.149 up to zero decimal places.
4	-2.475	-2.48	=ROUNDUP(A4, 2)	Rounds -2.475 to two decimal places.
5	57.5	60	=ROUNDUP(A5, -1)	Rounds 57.5 to one decimal place to the left of the decimal point.
6	671.3	700	=ROUNDUP(A6,-2)	Rounds 671.3 to two decimal places to the left of the decimal point.
7	1.78	2	=ROUNDUP(A7,0)	Rounds 1.78 up to zero decimal places.
8	-70.45	-100	=ROUNDUP(A8,-2)	Rounds -70.45 to the nearest multiple of 100.
9				
10				
11				
12				
13				

Formula explanations

=ROUNDUP(A2, 1)

In the formula above, A2 is the cell reference to the value to be rounded up. The num_digits argument is 1, specifying that we want to round up to 1 decimal place.

=ROUNDUP(A3, 0)

In the formula above, A3 is the cell reference to the value to round up. The num_digits argument is 0, specifying that we want to round up to a whole number, i.e., zero decimal places.

=ROUNDUP(A5, -1)

In the formula above, the num_digits argument is -1, specifying that we want to round up to one decimal place to the left of the decimal point. So, 57.5 is rounded up to 60.

ROUNDDOWN Function

The ROUNDDOWN function rounds a number down towards zero.

Syntax

=ROUNDDOWN(number, num_digits)

Arguments

Argument	Description
number	Required. The number you want to round down.
num_digits	Required. The number of decimal places you want to round the number down to.

Remarks

- ROUNDDOWN works like ROUND but always rounds a number down.
- Number is rounded down to the specified number of decimal places if num_digits is greater than 0 (zero).
- Number is rounded down to the nearest integer if num_digits is 0.
- Number is rounded down to the left of the decimal point if num_digits is less than 0.

Examples

In the following examples, ROUNDDOWN is applied to several values. The table displays the value, result, formula, and description.

	A	B	C	D
1	Value	Result	Formula text	Description
2	3.15	3.1	=ROUNDDOWN(A2, 1)	Rounds 3.15 down to one decimal place.
3	4.149	4	=ROUNDDOWN(A3, 0)	Rounds 4.149 down to zero decimal places.
4	-2.475	-2.47	=ROUNDDOWN(A4, 2)	Rounds -2.475 down to two decimal places.
5	57.5	50	=ROUNDDOWN(A5, -1)	Rounds 57.5 down to one decimal place to the left of the decimal point.
6	671.3	600	=ROUNDDOWN(A6,-2)	Rounds 671.3 down to the nearest multiple of 100.
7	1.78	1	=ROUNDDOWN(A7,0)	Rounds 1.78 down to zero decimal places.
8	-71.45	-70	=ROUNDDOWN(A8,-1)	Rounds -71.45 down to the nearest multiple of 10.
9				

Formula explanations

= ROUNDDOWN(A2, 1)

In the formula above, A2 is the cell reference holding the value to be rounded down. The num_digits argument is 1, specifying that we want to round down to 1 decimal place. So, 3.15 is rounded down to 3.1.

= ROUNDDOWN(A3, 0)

In the formula above, A3 is the cell reference to the value to round down. The num_digits argument is 0, specifying that we want to round down to a whole number, i.e., zero decimal places. So, 4.149 is rounded down to 4.

=ROUNDDOWN(A5, -1)

In the formula above, A5 is the cell reference to the value to round down. The num_digits argument is -1, specifying that we want to round down to one decimal place to the left of the decimal point. So, 57.5 is rounded down to 50.

Manipulating Text with Functions

The text functions in Excel can be found by going to **Formulas > Function Library > Text** on the ribbon. The dropdown menu lists all the text functions in Excel. Text functions are useful for manipulating and rearranging text values. For example, when you import data into Excel from other applications, you may encounter irregular text spacing or data with the wrong case. You may want to remove extra spaces from the data or change the case to uppercase or lowercase.

The functions in this section enable you to create formulas that can extract a substring from the left, right, or middle of a string. The newly introduced dynamic array text functions allow you to perform tasks for which you previously needed two or three functions.

 Tip The **Flash Fill** command on the Home tab enables you to automatically perform many text manipulation tasks for which you previously needed functions. To learn more about Flash Fill, see my Excel 2022 Basics book.

TEXTBEFORE Function

The TEXTBEFORE function returns text that occurs before a given delimiter or string. If multiple instances of a delimiter exist in the text, you can specify which instance to use for the text portion extraction. TEXTBEFORE offers the same functionality (and more) to handle tasks previously needing a combination of the LEFT and FIND functions.

Note This function is currently only available in Excel for Microsoft 365.

Syntax

=TEXTBEFORE(text,delimiter,[instance_num], [match_mode], [match_end], [if_not_found])

Arguments

Argument	Description
text	Required. A value or cell reference representing the text from which you want to extract a substring.
delimiter	Required. The character or text marking the point you want to extract text before.
instance_num	Optional. The instance of the delimiter marking the end point from which you want to extract the text. Use when *text* has more than one instance of *delimiter*, and you want an instance other than the first. The first delimiter instance is 1 (default), the second is 2, and so on. A negative number starts the search from the end.
match_mode	Optional. Determines if the delimiter match is case-sensitive. 0 = case-sensitive; 1= case-insensitive. The default is case-sensitive if omitted.
match_end	Optional. You can enable this option to treat the end of the text as the delimiter for instances where the delimiter is not found. 0 = disabled; 1 = Enabled The default is disabled if omitted.
if_not_found	Optional. Specifies the value to return if no match is found. If this argument is omitted and no match is found, the default returned is #N/A.

Remarks

- TEXTBEFORE returns a #VALUE! error if instance_num is 0 or greater than the length of text.

- TEXTBEFORE returns a #N/A error if the specified delimiter is not in text.

- TEXTBEFORE returns a #N/A error if the value entered for the instance_num argument exceeds the number of occurrences of delimiter in text.

Examples

The examples in the image below use TEXTBEFORE (in column B) to extract part of the string in column A. The formulas are shown in column C.

B2		fx	=TEXTBEFORE(A2," ")	
	A	B	C	D
1	**Text**	**Extracted text**	**Formula text**	**Description**
2	Linda Mitchell	Linda	=TEXTBEFORE(A2," ")	Finds space as delimiter
3	Christina Taylor, Analyst	Christina Taylor	=TEXTBEFORE(A3,",")	Finds comma as delimiter
4	Sanchez, Shawn, Manager	Sanchez, Shawn	=TEXTBEFORE(A4,",",2)	Find 2nd comma as delimiter
5	Andrew Steven James	Andrew Steven	=TEXTBEFORE(A5," ",2)	Finds 2nd space as delimiter
6	NWTCFV-91	NWTCFV	=TEXTBEFORE(A6,"-")	Finds dash as delimiter
7	Connecticut - CT	Connecticut	=TEXTBEFORE(A7," - ")	Finds dash and space
8	GTECH-365-4001	GTECH-365	=TEXTBEFORE(A8,"-",2)	Finds 2nd instance of dash
9	GTECH-365-4002-402	GTECH-365-4002	=TEXTBEFORE(A9,"-",-1)	Starts search from the end
10	15 x 45 x 30	15 x 45	=TEXTBEFORE(A10," x ",2)	Finds 2nd instance of x
11				
12				
13				

Formula explanations

=TEXTBEFORE(A2," ")

This formula has A2 as the text from which to extract a substring. The delimiter is a space specified by the double quotes.

=TEXTBEFORE(A3,",")

The delimiter here is a comma.

=TEXTBEFORE(A4,",",2)

The text is in A4, and the delimiter is a comma. The instance_num is 2, which matches the second instance of a comma.

=TEXTBEFORE(A7," - ")

The delimiter is a hyphen with a space on both sides.

=TEXTBEFORE(A8,"-",2)

The delimiter here is a hyphen, and we want to extract all text before the second instance of a hyphen.

=TEXTBEFORE(A9,"-",-1)

The delimiter here is a hyphen. The instance_num is -1, which searches for the first hyphen starting from the end of the text. The formula then returns all text before the hyphen.

=TEXTBEFORE(A10," x ",2)

The delimiter here is a lowercase x bordered by two spaces. The instance_num is 2, which means the formula finds the second instance of x and returns all text before it.

TEXTAFTER Function

The TEXTAFTER function returns text that occurs after a specified delimiter or substring. If multiple instances of a delimiter exist in the text, you can specify which instance to use for the text extraction. You can use TEXTAFTER in instances where you would have previously needed to combine the RIGHT, FIND, and LEN functions to achieve the same result.

Note This function is currently only available in Excel for Microsoft 365.

Syntax

=TEXTAFTER(text,delimiter,[instance_num], [match_mode], [match_end], [if_not_found])

Arguments

Argument	Description
text	Required. A value or cell reference representing the text from which you want to extract a substring.
delimiter	Required. This argument is a character or text marking the point after which you want to extract text.
instance_num	Optional. The instance of the delimiter marking the point after which you want to extract the text. Use when *text* has more than one instance of *delimiter,* and you want an instance other than the first. The first delimiter instance is 1 (default), the second is 2, and so on. A negative number starts the search from the end of the list.
match_mode	Optional. Determines if the delimiter match is case-sensitive. 0 = case-sensitive; 1= case-insensitive.

	The default is case-sensitive if omitted.
match_end	Optional. Treats the end of the text as the delimiter, for example, where the delimiter is not found.
	0 = disabled; 1 = Enabled.
if_not_found	Optional. Specifies the value to return if no match is found. If this argument is omitted and no match is found, the default returned is #N/A.

Remarks

- TEXTAFTER returns a #VALUE! error if instance_num is 0 or greater than the length of *text*.

- TEXTAFTER returns a #N/A error if the specified delimiter is not in *text*.

- TEXTAFTER will return a #N/A error if instance_num is greater than the number of instances of delimiter in *text*.

Examples

The examples in the image below use TEXTAFTER (in column B) to extract part of the string in column A. The formulas are displayed in column C.

	A	B	C	D
1	**Text**	**Extracted**	**Formula text**	**Description**
2	Linda Mitchell	Mitchell	=TEXTAFTER(A2," ")	Finds space as delimiter
3	Sanchez, Shawn	Shawn	=TEXTAFTER(A3,", ")	Find comma and space as delimiter
4	Delaware - DE	DE	=TEXTAFTER(A4," - ")	Finds dash and space
5	NWTCFV-91	91	=TEXTAFTER(A5,"-")	Finds dash as delimiter
6	GTX-365-PH	PH	=TEXTAFTER(A6,"-",2)	Finds 2nd instance of dash
7	15 ft x 10 ft	10 ft	=TEXTAFTER(A7," x ")	Finds x as delimiter
8	Andrew Steven James	Steven	=TEXTBEFORE(TEXTAFTER(A8," ")," ")	Returns text from the middle of the string
9	Minnesota (MN)	MN	=TEXTBEFORE(TEXTAFTER(A9,"("),")")	Returns the abbreviation without the brackets
10	Cora Fabric Chair	Chair	=TEXTAFTER(A10," ",-1)	Returns the first item from the right of the string
11	Habitat Oken Console Table	Table	=TEXTAFTER(A11," ",-1)	Returns the first item from the right of the string
12	Windsor 2 Seater Cuddle Chair	Chair	=TEXTAFTER(A12," ",-1)	Returns the first item from the right of the string
13	Fabric Chair in a Box	Box	=TEXTAFTER(A13," ",-1)	Returns the first item from the right of the string
14				
15				
16				

Formula explanations

=TEXTAFTER(A2," ")

In this formula, A2 is the cell reference to the text from which to extract a substring after the delimiter. The delimiter argument is a space character denoted by a space in quotes.

=TEXTAFTER(A3,", ")

A3 is the cell reference to the text from which to extract a substring after the delimiter. The delimiter argument is a comma and a space character.

=TEXTAFTER(A4," - ")

The delimiter here is a hyphen with a space on each side.

=TEXTAFTER(A5,"-")

The delimiter argument here is a hyphen with no spaces.

=TEXTAFTER(A6,"-",2)

The delimiter argument here is a hyphen. The instance_num is 2, which finds the second instance of a hyphen and returns all text after.

=TEXTAFTER(A7," x ")

The delimiter argument here is a lowercase x with a space character on each side.

=TEXTBEFORE(TEXTAFTER(A8," ")," ")

A8 = Andrew Steven James
Result = Steven

This formula combines TEXTBEFORE and TEXTAFTER to extract the middle name from a full name in cell A8. TEXTAFTER first selects the text after the first space, which is **Steven James**. TEXTBEFORE selects the name before the space in the returned result, **Steven**. This formula provides an easier solution than using the MID and FIND functions to achieve the same result.

=TEXTBEFORE(TEXTAFTER(A9,"("),")")

A9 = Minnesota (MN)
Result = MN

This formula combines TEXTBEFORE and TEXTAFTER to extract the abbreviation from the value in cell A9. TEXTAFTER first returns the text after the opening bracket **MN)**. TEXTBEFORE then returns the characters before the closing bracket, which is **MN**.

=TEXTAFTER(A10," ",-1)

The delimiter argument in the above formula is a space. The instance_num is -1, which tells Excel to find the last space in the text string and return the text after it.

TEXTSPLIT Function

The TEXTSPLIT function enables you to split text strings into different columns or rows. TEXTSPLIT is a dynamic array function that can take in one value and return multiple values. You can use the Text-to-Columns wizard in Excel for splitting text into columns, but TEXTSPLIT is easier to use and offers more splitting options.

 Note This function is currently only available in Excel for Microsoft 365.

Syntax

=TEXTSPLIT(text,col_delimiter,[row_delimiter],[ignore_empty], [match_mode], [pad_with])

Arguments

Argument	Description
text	Required. A value or cell reference representing the text you want to split.
col_delimiter	Required. The delimiter used to split the text into different columns.
row_delimiter	Optional. The delimiter used to split the text into different rows.
ignore_empty	Optional. Enter TRUE to ignore empty values, i.e., two or more consecutive delimiters without a value in-between them. Enter FALSE to create empty cells for empty values. FALSE is the default if this argument is omitted.
match_mode	Optional. Determines if case sensitivity is used to match the delimiter. Case sensitivity is used by default. 0 = case-sensitive (default). 1 = case-insensitive.
pad_with	Optional. A value to use for missing values in two-dimensional arrays. The default is #N/A.

Remarks:

If you set ignore_empty to TRUE, ensure there are no spaces between the consecutive delimiters. Otherwise, the feature to ignore empty values does not work.

Example 1 – Splitting into columns

The table below has examples of text being split into different columns using different delimiters.

Notice that you have to enter the delimiter precisely. For example, if there is a gap (or space) after a delimiter, you must enter that space after the delimiter in your formula to ensure blank spaces are not added to the split values. You can also use the TRIM function in your formula to remove any blank spaces from the result if the original text contains irregular spacing.

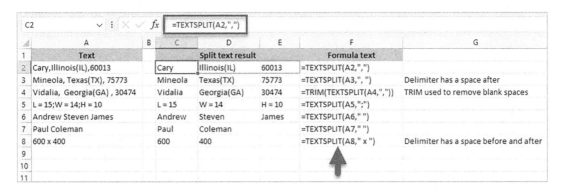

Example 2 – Splitting into rows

The example below splits the text in A13 into rows rather than columns. To split the text into rows, leave the col_delimiter argument empty, and enter the delimiter for the row_delimiter argument.

=TEXTSPLIT(A13,,", ")

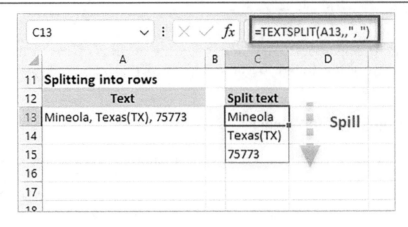

Example 3 – Splitting text with different delimiters

If the text values to be split have more than one delimiter type, you can use curly brackets to specify more than one delimiter for the col_delimiter argument. See the example below.

=TEXTSPLIT(A2,{",",";"})

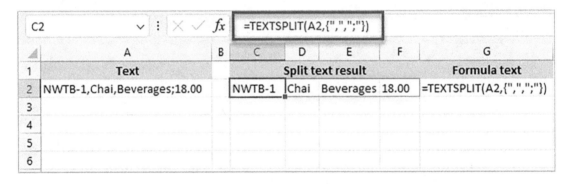

Example 4 – Two-dimensional splits

TEXTSPLIT allows you to split a text string into rows and columns simultaneously, where you specify delimiters for both the col_delimiter and row_delimiter arguments.

The example below splits the text in A2 into columns and rows by providing the following:

- The **col_delimiter** - an equal sign ("=")
- The **row_delimiter** - a semi-colon, and space "; "

The formula looks like this:

=TEXTSPLIT(A2,"=","; ")

The formula creates a 2D array made up of 2 columns and 3 rows:

C2		fx	=TEXTSPLIT(A2,"=","; ")		
	A	B	C		D
1	Text		Split text		
2	Chai=18.00; Syrup=10.00; Cajun Seasoning=22.00		Chai	18.00	
3			Syrup	10.00	
4			Cajun Seasoning	22.00	
5					
6					
7					

Example 5 – Handling empty values

In the example below, the text string to be split has empty values indicated by two or more consecutive delimiters. The formula below has been wrapped in TRIM to fix any inconsistent spacing.

By default, TEXTSPLIT will create empty cells for the missing values, as shown in the image below. You can also set the ignore_empty argument to FALSE to get the same result.

=TRIM(TEXTSPLIT(A2,",",""))

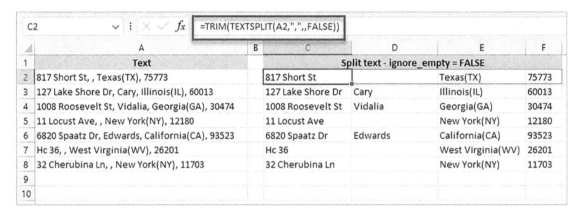

To ignore empty values, set the ignore_empty argument to TRUE, as shown in the formula below.

=TEXTSPLIT(A14,", ",,,TRUE)

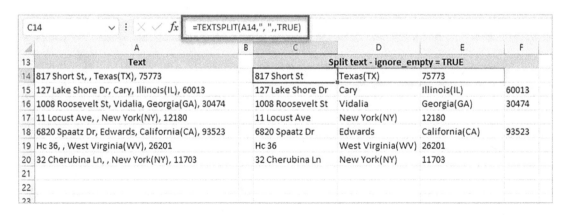

TEXTJOIN Function

TEXTJOIN is the opposite of TEXTSPLIT, as it enables you to combine text values from multiple cells into one string. The difference between TEXTJOIN and the CONCAT function is that TEXTJOIN has extra arguments that allow you to specify a delimiter as a separator. If your delimiter is a blank space, this function concatenates the ranges like CONCAT. This function also has options that allow you to ignore empty cells.

Syntax

=TEXTJOIN(delimiter, ignore_empty, text1, [text2], ...)

Arguments

Argument	Description
delimiter	Required. The character you want to use to separate text items in your string. The delimiter can be a string, one or more characters enclosed in double quotes, or a cell reference containing a text string. If this argument is a number, it will be treated as text.
ignore_empty	Required. Enter TRUE or FALSE. If the value is TRUE, Excel ignores empty cells.
text1	Required. The first text item to be joined. It can be a string, a cell reference, or a range with several cells.
[text2, ...]	Optional. Additional text items you want to join. You can have up to 252 arguments for the text items, including text1. Each can be a string, a cell reference, or a range with several cells.

Remarks

TEXTJOIN will return the #VALUE! error if the resulting string exceeds the cell limit of 32767 characters.

Example

In the following example, we use TEXTJOIN in C2:C7 to combine the First and Last name values from A2:A7 and B2:B7. The flexibility provided by TEXTJOIN enables us to swap the order of the names and separate them with a comma.

	A	B	C	D
1	**First name**	**Last name**	**Combined**	**Formula text**
2	Bruce	Henderson	Henderson, Bruce	=TEXTJOIN(", ", TRUE,B2,A2)
3	Louis	Anderson	Anderson, Louis	=TEXTJOIN(", ", TRUE,B3,A3)
4	Earl	Foster	Foster, Earl	=TEXTJOIN(", ", TRUE,B4,A4)
5	Sean	Hill	Hill, Sean	=TEXTJOIN(", ", TRUE,B5,A5)
6	Benjamin	Martinez	Martinez, Benjamin	=TEXTJOIN(", ", TRUE,B6,A6)
7	Joe	Perez	Perez, Joe	=TEXTJOIN(", ", TRUE,B7,A7)
8				
9	**Name**			
10	Bruce Henderson			
11	Louis Anderson			
12	Earl Foster			
13	Sean Hill			
14				
15	**Combined**			
16	Bruce Henderson, Louis Anderson, Earl Foster, Sean Hill			=TEXTJOIN(", ",TRUE,A10:A13)
17				

Explanation of formula

=TEXTJOIN(", ", TRUE,B2,A2)

The *delimiter* argument is a comma enclosed in quotes. The *ignore_empty* argument is TRUE because we want to ignore empty cells. The *text1* and *text2* arguments are cell references B2 and A2, representing the first and last names. The formula is copied to the other cells to populate the other results in the column.

Tip You can now use the **Flash Fill** command on the Excel ribbon to achieve the same results as above. It would be faster to use Flash Fill for this task in certain situations than a formula. If you want more information on Flash Fill, please see my book, *Excel Basics*.

=TEXTJOIN(", ",TRUE,A10:A13)

The second example uses the TEXTJOIN function to concatenate names in a range of cells (A10:A13) into a single string with a comma used as a separator.

CONCAT Function

The CONCAT function enables you to combine the text from multiple ranges or strings into one string. The function does not provide a delimiter, so you must add that manually in your formula. For example, =CONCAT("Hello"," ","world") will return *Hello world*. If you want to specify a delimiter, see the TEXTJOIN function.

Note This function was introduced as a replacement for the CONCATENATE function. CONCATENATE is still available in Excel for backward compatibility, but it is recommended that you use CONCAT going forward.

Syntax

=CONCAT(text1, [text2],…)

Arguments

Argument	Description
text1	Required. This argument represents a text item to be joined. It could be a string or a range of cells with text.
[text2, ...]	Optional. Additional text to be joined. You can have up to 253 arguments of text items to be joined. Each can be a string or a range of cells with text.

Remarks

- If the resulting string exceeds the cell limit of 32767 characters, CONCAT returns the #VALUE! error.

- You can use the TEXTJOIN function to include delimiters like spacing and/or commas between the texts you want to combine.

Example

In the example below, we used the CONCAT function differently to concatenate text from different cells.

	A	B	C	D	E
1	First name	Lastname		Result	Formula text
2	Bruce	Henderson		Bruce Henderson	=CONCAT(A2," ",B2)
3	Louis	Anderson		Bruce & Louis	=CONCAT(A2, " & ", A3)
4	Earl	Foster		Bruce and Louis did a good job.	=CONCAT(A2, " and ", A3, " did a good job.")
5				Anderson, Louis	=CONCAT(B3,", ",A3)
6				Anderson, Louis	=B3 & ", " & A3
7					
8					
9					

Explanation of formulas

=CONCAT(A2," ",B2)

This formula concatenates the text in A2 and B2 with an empty string in between, represented by the empty string in the formula.

=CONCAT(A2, " & ", A3)

This formula concatenates the text in cells A2 and A3 with an ampersand character (&) in the middle representing two first names.

=CONCAT(A2, " and ", A3, "did a good job.")

This formula uses the text in cells A2 and A3 to form part of a larger sentence.

=CONCAT(B3,", ",A3)

This formula concatenates the text in cells B3 and A3 with a comma in-between, representing the Last name and First name.

=B3 & ", " & A3

The formula above is for comparisons. It doesn't use CONCAT but achieves the same result using ampersands (Excel's concatenation operator).

FIND Function

The FIND function is used to locate the starting position of one text string within another. It returns the position of the first character of the text you're searching for within the second text. The search is case-sensitive.

Syntax

=FIND(find_text, within_text, [start_num])

Arguments

Argument	Description
find_text	Required. The text you want to find.
within_text	Required. The text string in which you want to find text.
start_num	Optional. Specifies the point from which you want to start the search in within_text. The first character in within_text is 1; the second is 2, etc.
	If you omit this argument, it will start from the first character in within_text.

Example 1

This example uses the FIND function to return the position of different characters in the string "United States." As shown in the results below, the FIND function is case-sensitive.

	A	B	C	D
1	Data			
2	United States			
3				
4	Search term	Result	Formula text	Explanation
5	Position of S	8	=FIND("S",$A$2)	Returns the position of uppercase S in United States
6	Position of s	13	=FIND("s",$A$2)	Returns the position of lowercase s in United States
7	Position of first t	4	=FIND("t",$A$2)	Returns the position of the first lowercase t in United States
8				
9				
10				
11				

Example 2

The FIND function is most useful when used as an argument in another function. In the following example, we combine FIND with RIGHT, LEFT, and LEN to perform different string extractions. The formulas use FIND to identify the divider's position, then LEFT/RIGHT extracts the portion of the required string.

G	H	I
Text	Result	Formula text
California - CA	California	=LEFT(G2,FIND("-",G2)-1)
Colorado - CO	Colorado	=LEFT(G3,FIND("-",G3)-1)
Connecticut - CT	Connecticut	=LEFT(G4,FIND("-",G4)-1)
Delaware - DE	DE	=RIGHT(G5,LEN(G5)-(FIND("-",G5)+1))
Florida - FL	FL	=RIGHT(G6,LEN(G6)-(FIND("-",G6)+1))
Georgia - GA	GA	=RIGHT(G7,LEN(G7)-(FIND("-",G7)+1))

=LEFT(G2,FIND("-",G2)-1)

FIND returns the position of "-", which is 12 in this case. We need to subtract 1 from this number to remove the divider from the part of the string we want to extract. The LEFT function then uses 10 as the starting point to return the characters in the string, starting from right to left. See the section **LEFT, RIGHT Functions** for more on the LEFT function.

LEFT and RIGHT Functions

The LEFT function returns the leftmost characters in a text string based on the number of characters you specify in one of its arguments. The RIGHT function returns the rightmost characters in a text string starting from the position you specify.

-💡-**Tip** You can now use the new TEXTBEFORE and TEXTAFTER functions to extract text more easily than you could with the LEFT and RIGHT functions.

Syntax

=LEFT(text, [num_chars])

=RIGHT(text,[num_chars])

Arguments

Argument	Description
text	Required. This argument represents the text string with the characters you want to extract.
num_chars	Optional. An integer that specifies the number of characters you want to extract from the text. The count starts from the left for the LEFT function and the right for the RIGHT function.

Remarks

- If *num_chars* is larger than the length of *text*, the functions will return all characters in *text*.

- If *num_chars* is omitted, the functions return only the first character for the LEFT function and only the last character for the RIGHT function.

Example

In the example below, we use the LEFT and RIGHT functions to extract portions of text in different ways.

	A	B	C
1	**Text**	**Result**	**Formula text**
2	Alabama - AL	A	=LEFT(A2)
3	Alaska - AK	K	=RIGHT(A3)
4	Arizona - AZ	Arizona	=LEFT(A4,7)
5	Arkansas - AR	AR	=RIGHT(A5,2)
6	California - CA	California	=LEFT(A6,FIND("-",A6)-1)
7	Colorado - CO	Colorado	=LEFT(A7,FIND("-",A7)-1)
8	Connecticut - CT	Connecticut	=LEFT(A8,FIND("-",A8)-1)
9	Delaware - DE	DE	=RIGHT(A9,LEN(A9)-(FIND("-",A9)+1))
10	Florida - FL	FL	=RIGHT(A10,LEN(A10)-(FIND("-",A10)+1))
11	Georgia - GA	GA	=RIGHT(A11,LEN(A11)-(FIND("-",A11)+1))
12	Quanta Builders	Quanta	=LEFT(A12, FIND(" ",A12)-1)
13			
14			

Formula explanations

=LEFT(A2)

In the formula above, cell A2 is the text argument. There is no num_chars argument. Thus, LEFT returns the first character on the left of the string.

=RIGHT(A3)

This formula has cell A3 as the text argument, and there is no num_chars argument. Hence, RIGHT returns the last character in the string.

=LEFT(A4,7)

This formula has cell A4 as the text argument and 7 as the num_chars argument. It returns **Arizona**, 7 characters from the left of the string.

=RIGHT(A5,2)

This formula takes cell A4 as the text argument and 7 as the num_chars argument. It returns **AR**, 2 characters from the right of the string.

=LEFT(A6,FIND("-",A6)-1)

This formula takes cell A6 as the text argument. We calculate the num_chars argument using the FIND function to find and return the position of the hyphen character (-) in the text.

We then subtract 1 from the result to return the number of characters in the text before the hyphen. Hence **FIND("-",A6)-1** will return 10. The result is California. This formula will work for any piece of text separated by a hyphen where we want to extract the left portion.

=RIGHT(A9,LEN(A9)-(FIND("-",A9)+1))

This formula takes cell A9 as the text argument. We calculate the num_chars argument by using FIND to return the position of the hyphen character (-) in the text. We then add 1 to move to the position of the first character after the hyphen (on the right).

The LEN function is used to get the length of the string as we want to subtract the number of characters returned by FIND to give us the number of characters after the hyphen, which is 2 in this case.

This formula will work for a piece of text of any length separated by a hyphen, regardless of the position of the hyphen.

=LEFT(A12, FIND(" ",A12)-1)

This formula uses LEFT to return the string before the first space. A12 is the cell containing the string from which we want to extract text. **FIND(" ",A12)-1** returns the number of characters before the first space.

LEFTB, RIGHTB Functions

LEFTB and RIGHTB are variants of the LEFT and RIGHT functions that return characters in a text string based on the number of bytes you specify.

RIGHTB/LEFTB are for systems set to a default language that supports the double-byte character set (DBCS). The languages that support DBCS include Japanese, Traditional Chinese, Simplified Chinese, and Korean. If your system has a default language that supports DBCS, you would have LEFTB and RIGHTB in place of LEFT and RIGHT.

If your system has a default language that supports the single-byte character set (SBCS), LEFTB/RIGHTB will behave the same as LEFT/RIGHT, counting 1 byte per character.

MID Function

The MID function extracts a portion of a text from another text based on a specified starting position and the number of characters to be extracted.

Tip For more complex text extractions, use the new TEXTBEFORE or TEXTAFTER functions. They're easier to use, offer more options, and can do most tasks you can do with MID.

Syntax

=MID(text, start_num, num_chars)

Arguments

Argument	Description
text	Required. A text string or a cell reference containing the characters you want to extract.
start_num	Required. A number that represents the starting point of the first character to extract from the value in *text*. The first character in *text* starts with 1. The second is 2, and so on.
num_chars	Required. A number specifying the number of characters you want to extract from *text*.

Remarks

- If the start_num argument is larger than the length of the string in the text argument, MID will return an empty text ("").
- MID will return the #VALUE! error if start_num is less than 1.
- MID returns the #VALUE! error if num_chars is a negative value.

Examples

The examples use the MID function to extract characters from several text values.

	A	B	C
1	**Text**	**Result**	**Formula text**
2	NWTCFV-91	NWTCFV	=MID(A2,1,LEN(A2)-3)
3	NWTCFV-90	90	=MID(A3,FIND("-",A3)+1,2)
4	NWT-100-CFV	100	=MID(A4,FIND("-",A4)+1,3)
5	01-345-4000	345	=MID(A5,4,3)
6	Andrew Steven James	Steven	=MID(A6,FIND(" ",A6)+1,FIND(" ",A6,FIND(" ",A6)+1)-FIND(" ",A6))
7	Minnesota(MN)	MN	=MID(A7,FIND("(",A7)+1,2)
8			
9			

Formula descriptions

=MID(A2,1,LEN(A2)-3)

Removes the last 3 characters in the text and returns the rest.

For this formula, A2 is the cell reference containing the string from which we want to extract text. We're starting from the first character, so start_num is 1. We want to return the length of the text except for the last 3 characters. We can use LEN to return this number for the num_chars argument.

=MID(A3,FIND("-",A3)+1,2)

Finds the hyphen in the text and returns the two characters after.

For this formula, A3 is the cell containing the string from which we want to extract text. We're starting from the first character after the hyphen "-", which we can identify with FIND("-",A3)+1. We want to return two characters, so 2 is the *num_chars* argument.

=MID(A5,4,3)

For this formula, A5 is the cell containing the string from which we want to extract characters. The first character to extract is 3, which starts at the fourth position, so we have 4 as our start_num. We want to return three characters, so we have 3 as the num_chars.

=MID(A6,FIND(" ",A6)+1,FIND(" ",A6,FIND(" ",A6)+1)-FIND(" ",A6))

This formula extracts the middle name from the full name.

The **text** argument is A6.

The **start_num** argument is FIND(" ",A6)+1. This nested formula identifies the position of the first character after the first space, which is 8.

The **num_chars** argument is FIND(" ",A6,FIND(" ",A6)+1)-FIND(" ",A6).

FIND(" ",A6,FIND(" ",A6)+1) finds the position of the second space, which is 14, and **FIND(" ",A6)** finds the position of the first space, which is 7.

We then subtract the position of the first space from the position of the second space like this **FIND(" ",A6,FIND(" ",A6)+1)-FIND(" ",A6)**, which is 14-7.

=MID(A7,FIND("(",A7)+1,2)

This formula finds the opening bracket in a string and returns the two characters after the bracket.

A7 is the cell containing the string from which we want to extract two characters. Our start_num is the position of the first character after the opening bracket "(", which we can identify with FIND("-",A3)+1. We want to return two characters, so 2 is the num_chars argument.

Performing Financial Calculations with Functions

You can access financial functions in Excel by clicking the Financial button, in the Function Library group, on the Formulas tab. Most of the financial functions in Excel are specialized functions used for financial accounting.

Definitions

Most of the financial functions in Excel have arguments that are acronyms for financial terms. For example, terms like PV (Present Value), FV (Future Value), PMT (Payment), and IPMT (interest payment) show up as arguments in many functions. It is important to understand the terminology to better understand these functions. The following section covers some key terms used.

Annuity

An annuity is a series of regular cash payments over a certain period. For example, a mortgage or a car loan is an annuity. An investment that pays regular dividends is also an annuity. Most of the functions covered in this chapter are known as annuity functions.

PV (Present Value)

PV is the present value of an investment based on a constant growth rate. It is the lump-sum amount that a series of future payments is worth right now.

FV (Future Value)

FV is the future value of an investment based on a constant rate of growth. Imagine a scenario where you need to save $25,000 to pay for a project in 20 years. In that case,

$25,000 is the future value. To calculate how much you need to save monthly, you'll also need to factor in an assumed interest rate over the period.

PMT (Payment)

PMT is the payment made for each period in the annuity. Usually, the payment includes the principal plus interest (without any other fees) set over the life of the annuity. For example, a $100,000 mortgage over 25 years at 3% interest would have monthly payments of $474. You would enter -474 into the formula as the *pmt*.

RATE

RATE is the interest rate per period. For example, a loan at a 6% annual interest rate will have an interest rate of 6%/12 per month.

NPER (Number of periods)

NPER is the number of payment periods for a loan or investment based on constant periodic payments and a constant interest rate. For example, a three-year loan with monthly payments will have 36 periods (3 x 12). Hence, the *nper* argument would be 3*12 for such a scenario.

Note The FV, PV, and PMT arguments can be positive or negative, depending on whether you are paying or receiving money. The values will be negative if you're paying out money and positive if you're receiving money.

PV Function

The PV function calculates the present value of an investment (or a loan), assuming a constant interest rate. The present value is the amount a series of future payments is currently worth. You can use PV with regular payments (such as a mortgage or other loan), periodic payments, or the future value of a lump sum paid now.

Syntax

=PV(rate, nper, pmt, [fv], [type])

Arguments

See the Definitions section above for a more detailed description of these arguments.

Arguments	Description
rate	Required. The interest rate per period.
nper	Required. The total number of payment periods in an annuity.
pmt	Required. The payment made for each period in the annuity.
	If you omit *pmt*, you must include the *fv* argument.
fv	Optional. This argument is the future value of an investment based on an assumed rate of growth.
	If you omit fv, it is assumed to be 0 (zero). For example, the future value of a loan is 0. If you omit fv, then you must include the pmt argument.
type	Optional. This argument is 0 or 1 and indicates when payments are due.
	0 or omitted = at the end of the period.
	1 = at the beginning of the period.

Remarks

- You must always specify the rate argument in the same units as the nper argument. For example, say you have monthly payments on a three-year loan at 5% annual interest. If you use 5%/12 for *rate*, you must use 3*12 for *nper*. If the payments on the same loan are being made annually, then you would use 5% for rate and 3 for nper.

- In annuity functions, the cash paid out (like a payment to savings) is represented by a negative number. The cash received (like a dividend payment) is represented by a positive number. For example, a $500 deposit would be represented by -500 for the depositor and by 500 for the bank.

Example

In the example below, we use the PV formula to calculate:

1. The present value of a $500 monthly payment over 25 years at a rate of 1.5% interest.

2. The present value of the lump sum that is needed now to create $20,000 in 10 years at a rate of 3.5% interest.

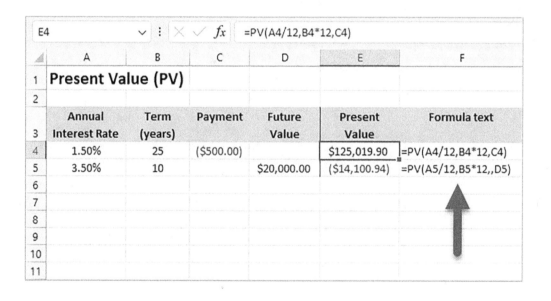

	A	B	C	D	E	F
E4			fx	=PV(A4/12,B4*12,C4)		
1	**Present Value (PV)**					
2						
3	**Annual Interest Rate**	**Term (years)**	**Payment**	**Future Value**	**Present Value**	**Formula text**
4	1.50%	25	($500.00)		$125,019.90	=PV(A4/12,B4*12,C4)
5	3.50%	10		$20,000.00	($14,100.94)	=PV(A5/12,B5*12,,D5)
6						
7						
8						
9						
10						
11						

Explanation of Formulas:

=PV(A4/12,B4*12,C4)

As you've probably noticed, the units for *rate* and *nper* have been kept consistent by specifying them in monthly terms, A4/12 and B4*12. The payment (pmt) has been entered in the worksheet as a negative value as this is money being paid out.

=PV(A5/12,B5*12,,D5)

The present value is a negative number as it shows the amount of cash that needs to be invested today (paid out) to generate the future value of $20,000 in 10 years at a rate of 3.5% interest.

FV Function

The FV function calculates an investment's future value (at a specified date in the future) based on a constant interest rate. You can use FV to calculate the future value of regular, periodic, or a single lump-sum payment.

Syntax

=FV(rate,nper,pmt,[pv],[type])

Arguments

Arguments	Description
rate	Required. The interest rate per period.
nper	Required. The total number of payment periods.
pmt	Required. The payment made for each period in the annuity.
	If you omit pmt, you must include pv.
pv	Optional. The present value of an investment based on a constant growth rate.
	If you omit pv, it is assumed to be 0 (zero), and you must include pmt.
type	Optional. The *type* is 0 or 1, indicating when payments are due.
	0 (or omitted) = at the end of the period.
	1 = at the beginning of the period.

Remarks

- You must always specify the rate argument in the same units as the nper argument. For example, say you have monthly payments on a three-year loan at 5% annual interest. If you use 5%/12 for *rate*, you must use 3*12 for *nper*. If the payments on the same loan are being made annually, then you would use 5% for rate and 3 for nper.

149

- In annuity functions, the cash paid out (like a payment to savings) is represented by a negative number. The cash received (like a dividend payment) is represented by a positive number. For example, a $500 deposit would be represented by -500 for the depositor and by 500 for the bank.

Example

The example below uses the FV function to calculate:

1. The future value of a monthly payment of $200 over 10 months at an interest of 6% per annum.

2. The future value of a lump sum of $1,000 plus 12 monthly payments of $100 at an interest rate of 6%.

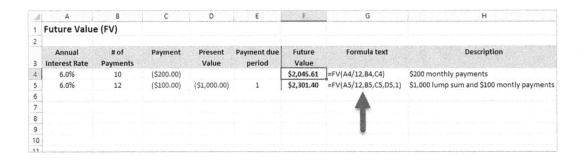

	A	B	C	D	E	F	G	H
1	Future Value (FV)							
2								
3	Annual Interest Rate	# of Payments	Payment	Present Value	Payment due period	Future Value	Formula text	Description
4	6.0%	10	($200.00)			$2,045.61	=FV(A4/12,B4,C4)	$200 monthly payments
5	6.0%	12	($100.00)	($1,000.00)	1	$2,301.40	=FV(A5/12,B5,C5,D5,1)	$1,000 lump sum and $100 montly payments
6								
7								
8								
9								
10								

Explanation of Formulas:

=FV(A4/12,B4,C4)

Note that the *rate* argument has been divided by 12 to represent monthly payments. The *pmt* argument is a negative value (C4) as this is money being paid out.

=FV(A5/12,B5,C5,D5,1)

This formula has the pmt argument and the optional pv argument, which represents the present value of the investment. The payment due period is 1, which means the payment starts at the beginning of the period.

NPV Function

The NPV function calculates the net present value, which is the present value of cash inflows and cash outflows over a period. It calculates the present value of an investment by applying a discount rate and a series of future payments that may be income (positive values) or payments/losses (negative values).

Syntax

=NPV(rate,value1,[value2],...)

Arguments

Argument	Description
Rate	Required. This argument is the percentage rate of discount over the length of the investment.
Value1	Required. This argument represents either a payment/loss (negative value) or income (positive value).
value2, ...	Optional. You can have additional values representing payments and income up to 254 value arguments.
	The length of time between these payments must be equally spaced and occur at the end of each period.

Remarks

- The rate argument in the function might represent the rate of inflation or the interest rate you might get from an alternative form of investment, such as a high-yield savings account.

- The value arguments represent the projected income (or loss) values over the period of the investment.

- Ensure you enter the payment and income values in the correct order because NPV uses the order of the value arguments to interpret the order of cash flows.

- The NPV investment begins one period before the date of the first cash flow (value1) and ends with the last cash flow (valueN) in the list of value arguments. If

151

the first cash flow happens at the beginning of the period, you must add it to the result of the NPV function and not include it as one of its value arguments.

- The main difference between NPV and PV is that with PV, the cash flows can start at the beginning or end of the period, while for NPV, the cash flows start at the beginning of the period. Also, PV has the same cash flow amount throughout the investment, while NPV can have different cash flow amounts.

- Arguments that are not numbers are ignored.

Example

The example below calculates the net present value of an initial investment of $50,000 over five years, considering an annual discount rate of 2.5 percent.

A4				fx	=NPV(I4,C4:G4)+B4				
	A	B	C	D	E	F	G	H	I
1	Net Present Value - 5 Year Investment								
2									
3	NPV	Initial cost of investment	Year 1 Return	Year 2 Return	Year 3 Return	Year 4 Return	Year 5 Return		Annual discount rate
4	$46,727.78	($50,000.00)	($1,000.00)	$15,000.00	$22,500.00	$30,000.00	$40,000.00		2.50%
5									
6									
7									
8									
9									

Formula explanation

=NPV(I4,C4:G4)+B4

In the figure above, Year 1 of the investment shows a loss of $1,000. Hence, Year 1 has been entered as a negative value. The other years of the investment (years two to five) returned profits, which were entered as positive values.

The function uses two arguments: the *rate* and *value1*, which references cells C4:G4. The initial investment is added to the result returned by the function rather than being an argument in the function.

The result shows the investment's net present value over five years is $46,727.78.

PMT Function

The PMT function calculates the payment of a loan on regular payments and a constant interest rate over a period. The PMT function is often used to calculate the repayment of a mortgage with a fixed interest rate.

Syntax

=PMT(rate, nper, pv, [fv], [type])

Arguments

Arguments	Description
rate	Required. The interest rate per period.
nper	Required. The total number of payment periods.
pv	Required. This argument is the present value of a principal or a series of future payments.
fv	Optional. This argument is the future value of an investment based on an assumed growth rate.
	If you omit fv, it is assumed to be 0 (zero), i.e., the future value of a loan is 0.
type	Optional. This argument is 0 or 1 and indicates when payments are due.
	0 (or omitted) = at the end of the period.
	1 = at the beginning of the period.

Remarks

- The payment returned by PMT is for the principal and interest. It does not include taxes, reserve payments, or other loan fees.

- You must always specify the *rate* argument in the same units as the *nper* argument. For example, say you have monthly payments on a three-year loan at 5% annual interest. If you use 5%/12 for *rate*, you must use 3*12 for *nper*. If the payments on the same loan are being made annually, then you would use 5% for rate and 3 for nper.

-ϙ-**Tip** To calculate the total amount paid over the duration of the loan, simply multiply the value returned by PMT by the number of payments (nper).

Example

In the example below, we calculate the PMT for two loans:

- A $10,000 loan over 12 payments at 8.0 percent interest.

- A $10,000 loan over 60 payments at 4.9 percent interest.

	A	B	C	D	E
1	**Payment (PMT)**				
2					
3	**Annual Interest Rate**	**# of payments**	**Loan amount**	**PMT**	**Formula text**
4	8.0%	12	$10,000.00	($869.88)	=PMT(A4/12,B4,C4)
5	4.9%	60	$10,000.00	($188.25)	=PMT(A5/12,B5,C5)
6					
7					
8					
9					
10					

Formula explanation

=PMT(A4/12,B4,C4)

The rate argument is the value in cell A4 divided by 12 to represent the interest rate in monthly terms because nper (in cell B4) is also specified in monthly terms. The pv argument is C4, which is the present value of the loan, $10,000.

Result: A monthly payment of $869.88 pays the loan off in 12 months.

=PMT(A5/12,B5,C5)

This formula is also for a loan of $10,000. However, the nper is 60, and the rate is 4.9 percent.

Result: A monthly payment of $188.25 pays the loan off in 60 months (5 years).

SLN Function

The SLN function is a depreciation function and calculates the straight-line depreciation of an asset over a period. It depreciates the asset by the same amount each year.

Syntax

=SLN(cost, salvage, life)

Arguments

Argument	Description
cost	Required. The initial cost of the depreciating asset.
salvage	Required. The value at the end of the depreciation (also referred to as the salvage value of the asset).
life	Required. The number of periods over which the asset is depreciating (also known as the useful life of the asset).

Example

In the example below, we have a report calculating the SLN depreciation of a couple of cars with a useful life of 10 years.

E4		⌄ ⋮ ✕ ✓ *fx*	=SLN(B4,D4,C4)		

	A	B	C	D	E	F
1	**Company car - straight-line depreciation (SLN)**					
2						
3	**Car**	**Cost**	**Yrs of useful life**	**Salvage value**	**Yearly depreciation allowance**	**Formula text**
4	Car 1	$20,000.00	10	$2,500.00	$1,750.00	=SLN(B4,D4,C4)
5	Car 2	$30,000.00	10	$7,500.00	$2,250.00	=SLN(B5,D5,C5)
6	Car 3	$45,000.00	10	$10,000.00	$3,500.00	=SLN(B6,D6,C6)
7						
8						
9						
10						
11						

Formula explanation

=SLN(B4,D4,C4)

In the formula above for **Car 1**, the cost references cell B4 ($20,000). The salvage value references cell D4 ($2,500). The life is C4 (10 years).

The formula returns $1,750, which is the yearly depreciation allowance to be made for the car. When listing this asset on the company's balance sheet, this value would be subtracted from the car's value.

The formula in E4 was copied down using the cell's fill handle to calculate the SLN value of the other cars on the list.

SYD Function

The SYD function (sum of years' digits) is a depreciation function that returns an asset's sum-of-years' digits depreciation over a specified period.

Syntax

=SYD(cost, salvage, life, per)

Arguments

Argument	Description
cost	Required. The initial cost of the asset you're depreciating.
salvage	Required. The value at the end of the depreciation (also referred to as the salvage value of the asset).
life	Required. The number of periods over which the asset is depreciated (also referred to as the useful life of the asset).
per	Required. The period for which to calculate the depreciation. It must be in the same units as life. For example, the period for the third year of an asset with a ten-year life will be 3.

Example

In the example below, we use the SYD function to calculate the depreciation of some office equipment over 10 years.

Function arguments:

- Cost = $40,000
- Life = 10 (years)
- Salvage = $1,000

B9		⌄ ⦂ ✕ ✓ *fx*	=SYD(InitialCost,SalvageValue,Life,A9)		
	A	B	C	D	E	F
1	Depreciation of office equipment - SYD					
2						
3	Initial Cost	$40,000.00		InitialCost = B3		
4	Life (years)	10		Life = B4		
5	Salvage value	$1,000.00		SalvageValue = B5		
6						
7	Year	SYD	Asset value			
8	0	$0.00	$40,000.00			
9	1	$7,090.91	$32,909.09			
10	2	$6,381.82	$26,527.27			
11	3	$5,672.73	$20,854.55			
12	4	$4,963.64	$15,890.91			
13	5	$4,254.55	$11,636.36	Cumulative		
14	6	$3,545.45	$8,090.91	depreciation		
15	7	$2,836.36	$5,254.55			
16	8	$2,127.27	$3,127.27			
17	9	$1,418.18	$1,709.09			
18	10	$709.09	$1,000.00			
19						

Formula explanation

=SYD(InitialCost,SalvageValue,Life,A9)

The formula in cell B9 uses the following range names for the cost, salvage, and life arguments:

- InitialCost = B3
- Life = B4
- SalvageValue = B5

The values in the cells above remain the same over the 10-year depreciation period, so using range names makes it easier to copy the formula for the other years. The *per* argument is a relative reference, cell A9, which changes with the year being calculated.

As depicted in the image above, with the SYD function, the depreciation amount gets progressively smaller compared to an SLN depreciation, for example, which is constant over the period.

=C8-SYD(InitialCost,SalvageValue,Life,A9)

The formulas in the **Asset value** column (C9:C18) subtract each year's depreciation from the previous year's calculated asset value. Hence, this column shows a progressive decrease in the asset's value over the 10-year period until it reaches the salvage value.

DB Function

The DB function is a depreciation function that uses the fixed-declining balance method to return the depreciation of an asset over a specified period. The fixed-declining balance method calculates the depreciation at a fixed rate.

Syntax

=DB(cost, salvage, life, period, [month])

Arguments

Arguments	Descriptions
cost	Required. The initial cost of the depreciating asset.
salvage	Required. The value at the end of the depreciation (also referred to as the salvage value of the asset).
life	Required. The number of periods over which the asset is depreciating (also referred to as the useful life of the asset).
period	Required. The period in the asset's life for which to calculate the depreciation. The period must be in the same units as life.
month	Optional. The number of months in the first year of the depreciation if it is not 12. If this argument is omitted, the default is 12.

159

Remarks

- The following formulas are used to calculate depreciation for a period:

  (cost - total depreciation from prior periods) * rate

  Where:

  rate = 1 - ((salvage / cost) ^ (1 / life))

- DB uses different formulas to calculate the depreciation for the first and last periods.

  First period:

  cost * rate * month / 12

  Last period:

  ((cost - total depreciation from prior periods) * rate * (12 - month)) / 12

Example 1

In the following example, we're calculating the depreciation of an asset over 5 years using the following data:

Argument	Value
Costs	$10,000
Salvage value	$2,000
Life	5 years

The first year has 12 months, so we can omit the month argument.

The formula for the **first year** will be thus:

=DB(10000, 2000, 5, 1)

Result: $2,750.00

Example 2

The following example calculates the depreciation of an asset with the following parameters:

Parameter	Value
Costs	$10,000
Salvage value	$2,000
Life (years)	5
Period (year)	5th year
First year (months)	8

The depreciation is calculated for the fifth year, and there are 8 months in the first year:

=DB(10000, 2000, 5, 5, 8)

Result: $855.84

Example 3

In this example, we use the SYD function to calculate the depreciation of office equipment with a useful life of 10 years. The initial cost is $40,000, and the salvage value is $1,000.

The first year has only 7 months, so we need to specify that in the *month* argument.

B9		⌄	: ✕ ✓ *fx*	=DB(InitialCost,Salvage,Life,A9,FirstYr)	

◢	A	B	C	D	E
1	**Depreciation of office equipment - (DB)**				
2					
3	Initial Cost	$40,000.00		*InitialCost = B3*	
4	Life (years)	10		*Life = B4*	
5	Salvage value	$1,000.00		*Salvage = B5*	
6	First Yr (# of months)	7		*FirstYr = B6*	
7					
8	**Year**	**DB**	**Asset value**		
9	1	$7,186.67	$32,813.33		
10	2	$10,106.51	$22,706.83		
11	3	$6,993.70	$15,713.12		
12	4	$4,839.64	$10,873.48		
13	5	$3,349.03	$7,524.45		
14	6	$2,317.53	$5,206.92		
15	7	$1,603.73	$3,603.19		
16	8	$1,109.78	$2,493.41		
17	9	$767.97	$1,725.44		
18	10	$531.43	$1,194.00		
19					

Formula explanation

=DB(InitialCost,Salvage,Life,A9,FirstYr)

The formula in cell B9 uses the following range names:

- InitialCost = B3
- Salvage = B4
- Life = B5
- FirstYr = B6

The range names correspond to the *cost, salvage, life,* and *month* arguments, as these remain the same over the 10-year depreciation period. The *per* argument is a relative reference, which changes in column A according to the year being calculated.

The *month* argument, FirstYr, holds a value of 7. This value specifies that the first year of the depreciation is 7 months rather than 12. This argument could have been omitted if the first year was 12 months.

From the image above, we can see that apart from the first year (7 months), the depreciation progresses linearly as the asset value reduces.

DDB Function

This DDB function returns the depreciation of an asset for a specified period using the double-declining balance method. The double-declining balance method calculates depreciation at an accelerated rate, with the depreciation highest in the first period and decreasing in successive periods.

This function is flexible, as you can change the *factor* argument if you don't want to use the double-declining balance method.

Syntax

=DDB(cost, salvage, life, period, [factor])

Arguments

Argument	Description
cost	Required. The initial cost of the depreciating asset.
salvage	Required. The value at the end of the depreciation (also referred to as the salvage value of the asset).
life	Required. The number of periods over which the asset is depreciating (also referred to as the useful life of the asset).
period	Required. The period in the asset's life for which to calculate the depreciation. It must be in the same units as life.
factor	Optional. The rate at which the balance declines.
	If omitted, the factor is assumed to be 2, which is the double-declining balance method.

Remarks

- The five arguments must be positive numbers.
- The DDB function uses the following formula to calculate depreciation for a period:

Min((cost - total depreciation from prior periods) * (factor/life), (cost - salvage - total depreciation from prior periods))

Example

In the following example, we use different DDB formulas to return results for the depreciation of a car.

Data:

- Initial Cost: $25,000.00

- Salvage value: $2,500.00

- Life (in years): 10

	A	B	C	D
1	**Depreciation of car - DDB**			
2				
3	Initial Cost	$25,000.00		
4	Salvage value	$2,500.00		
5	Life (in years)	10		
6				
7	**Period**	**Depreciation**	**Formula text**	
8	First day	$13.70	=DDB(Cost,Salvage,LifeInYrs*365,1)	*Factor 2 (default)*
9	First month	$416.67	=DDB(Cost,Salvage,LifeInYrs*12,1)	
10	First year	$5,000.00	=DDB(Cost,Salvage,LifeInYrs,1)	
11	First year (factor of 1.5)	$3,750.00	=DDB(Cost,Salvage,LifeInYrs,1,1.5)	*For comparisons*
12	Tenth year	$671.09	=DDB(Cost,Salvage,LifeInYrs,10)	
13				
14	*Cost = B3*			
15	*Salvage = B4*			
16	*LifeInYrs = B5*			
17				

Explanation of formulas

=DDB(Cost,Salvage,LifeInYrs*365,1)

The above formula uses range names for cell references:

- Cost = B3

- Salvage = B4
- LifeInYrs = B5

These range names relate to the *cost*, *salvage*, and *life* arguments in the formula.

Life is (10 * 365) because we want to calculate the depreciation in daily units rather than months or years. The period is 1, representing the first day of the item's life. The factor argument is omitted, so it defaults to 2, using the double-declining balance method.

=DDB(Cost,Salvage,LifeInYrs*12,1,2)

The formula above calculates the first month's depreciation. The factor argument was included in this case to specify the double-declining balance method. However, omitting the factor defaults to 2.

=DDB(Cost,Salvage,LifeInYrs,1)

The first year's depreciation. Notice that the *life* argument LifeInYrs has not been multiplied by 12, so the formula will return a result for year 1 as specified in the period argument.

=DDB(Cost,Salvage,LifeInYrs,1,1.5)

This formula is the first year's depreciation using a factor of 1.5 instead of the double-declining balance method.

=DDB(Cost,Salvage,LifeInYrs,10)

The above formula returns the tenth year's depreciation calculation. Factor has been omitted, so it defaults to 2.

Installing the Analysis ToolPak

The Excel Analysis ToolPak is an add-on that you can install that enables you to carry out complex statistical or engineering analyses. You can save a lot of time as you simply provide the data and parameters, and the tool uses the appropriate engineering or statistical functions to calculate and display the results in output tables. Some of the tools even generate charts in addition to output tables.

You can only use the data analysis functions on one worksheet at a time. When you carry out data analysis on a group of worksheets at the same time, results will appear on the first worksheet, and empty tables will appear on the remaining worksheets. To carry out the data analysis on the rest of the worksheets, you'll need to recalculate the analysis tool for each worksheet.

Follow these steps to install the Analysis ToolPak:

1. Select **File** > **Excel Options** (or press Alt+FT to directly open the Excel Options dialog box), and then click **Add-Ins**.

    The Add-Ins tab lists all the names, locations, and types of the add-ins currently available to you in Excel.

2. In the **Manage box** (at the bottom of the Add-ins tab), select **Excel Add-ins** and then click **Go**.

    If you're on a Mac, in the file menu, go to **Tools** > **Excel Add-ins**.

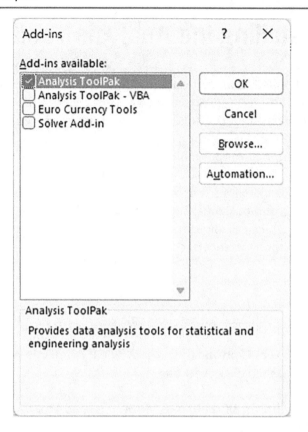

3. In the **Add-Ins** dialog box, select the **Analysis ToolPak** check box, and then click **OK**.

4. To access the Analysis ToolPak tools on the Excel ribbon, click the **Data** tab, then in the **Analysis** group, click the **Data Analysis** button.

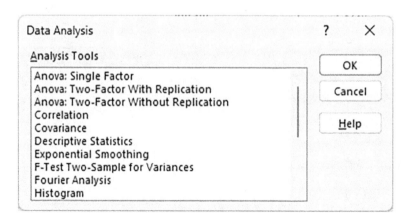

Notes:

- If Analysis ToolPak is not listed in the Add-Ins box, click **Browse** to find it on your computer. You may get a prompt saying that the Analysis ToolPak is not currently installed on your computer. Click **Yes** to install it.

- (Optional) To include the Visual Basic for Application (VBA) functions for the Analysis ToolPak, select the **Analysis ToolPak - VBA** check box. This is only required if you intend to use VBA code in your data analysis.

Chapter 6

Use Macros to Automate Excel Tasks

This chapter will cover the following:

- How to record and run macros in Excel.
- Adding macro command buttons on the ribbon.
- Assigning a macro to a graphic object in your worksheet.
- Macro security, including the Trust Center and Trusted Locations.
- How to view and edit your macros in the Visual Basic Editor.

Macros enable you to automate pretty much any task you can manually carry out in Excel. You can use Excel's macro recorder to record tasks you perform routinely. Macros enable you to do the work faster, as Excel can play back keystrokes and mouse actions much faster than when you perform them manually. Also, a macro ensures a particular task is performed in a consistent way, which reduces the likelihood of errors.

Excel uses the Visual Basic for Applications (VBA) programming language to record all the commands and keystrokes you make while recording the macro. VBA is a programming language developed and used primarily for Microsoft 365 applications like Access, Word, Excel, PowerPoint, etc. You don't need to have any knowledge of VBA to record and use macros in Excel, but you can use the Visual Basic Editor to view and edit your macros after recording them if needed.

Overview

There are two ways you can create a macro in Excel:

1. You can use Excel's macro recorder to record your actions as you perform a task in the worksheet.

2. Use the VBA editor to write the code that performs the task from scratch. VBA programming is outside the scope of this book, but we will briefly look at the code editor.

Whichever method you use, Excel will create a special code module that holds the actions and instructions recorded in the macro. These are stored as Visual Basic code. In fact, one way to create VBA code for Excel is to start the macro recorder and manually perform the task for which you want to write code. Then you open the macro in the Visual Basic Editor and put the finishing touches to the code. This method is how developers can quickly create code to automate Excel.

Displaying the Developer Tab

A default installation of Excel does not add the **Developer** tab to the ribbon. When working with macros and the Visual Basic Editor, it is much easier to access commands on the Developer tab.

Follow the steps below to display the **Developer** tab on the ribbon (if it is not already added):

1. Right-click anywhere on the ribbon (below the buttons) and select **Customize the Ribbon**. You can also open the Excel Options dialog box by selecting **File > Options > Customize Ribbon**.

    Excel opens the **Customize the Ribbon** pane in the Excel Options dialog box.

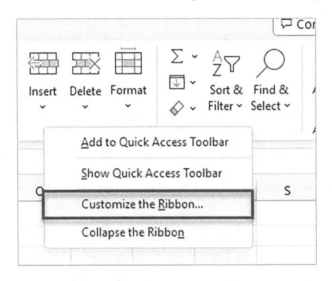

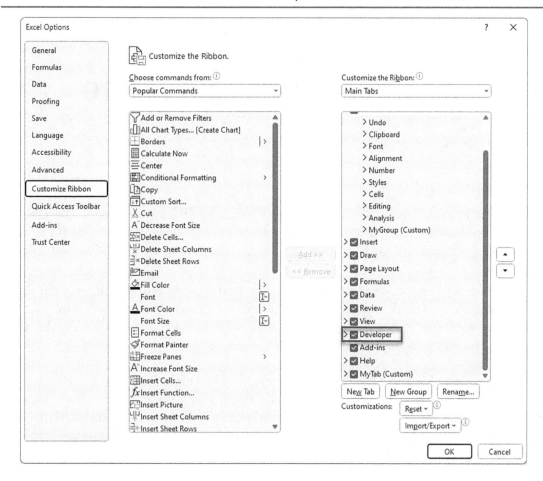

2. On the right side of the dialog box, select **Main Tabs** in the dropdown list. Select the **Developer** check box in the list below.

3. Click **OK**.

☀️-Tip

For more on customizing the Excel ribbon, see my Excel 2022 Basics book.

Where to Store Your Macro

You can store macros in the following locations:

- The current workbook.
- A new workbook.
- The Personal Macro Workbook (PERSONAL.XLSB). This is a hidden workbook stored in the XLSTART folder on your computer. This workbook is available to all workbooks on the computer.

When you record and store a macro in the **Personal Macro Workbook**, you can run it from any open workbook. Macros saved as part of the current workbook can only be run inside that workbook. When recording a macro, you get to select where to save it, the name of the macro, and what keyboard shortcut to assign to it.

When assigning a keyboard shortcut to a macro, you can assign the **Ctrl** key plus a letter from A-Z. For example, Ctrl+M. You can also use Ctrl+Shift and a letter from A-Z, for example, Ctrl+Shift+M. You can't assign some keyboard shortcut, for instance, Ctrl+ (any number) or Ctrl+ (a punctuation mark). Also, you should avoid using known Windows shortcut keys like Ctrl+C or Ctrl+V (the shortcut keys for copy and paste).

How to Start the Macro Recorder

There are three ways you can start the macro recorder in Excel:

- **From the Status bar**

  On the Excel Status bar, click the **Record Macro** button (bottom left of the window, next to the Ready indicator). Having the Record Macro button on the status bar is convenient as it means you don't have to switch from your current tab on the ribbon to start and stop the recording.

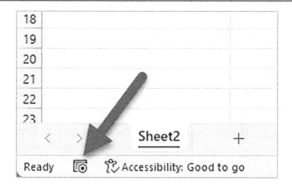

- **From the View tab**

  On the **View** tab, click the dropdown arrow on the **Macros** button, and then select **Record Macro** from the dropdown menu.

- **From the Developer tab**

  On the **Developer** tab, click the **Record Macro** command button.

View Tab Macro Options

On the **View** tab of the ribbon, the **Macros** button has three options on its dropdown list (you can also find these options as command buttons in the Code group in the Developer tab):

- **View Macros**: This opens the **Macro** dialog box, which enables you to select and run a macro that has already been recorded. You can also choose to edit macros from here.

- **Record Macro**: This opens the **Record Macro** dialog box, which allows you to define settings for the macro you want to record and start the macro recorder.

- **Use Relative References**: This setting, which you can turn on before recording a macro, uses relative cell references when recording macros. Using relative cell references makes the macro more flexible because it enables you to run it anywhere on the worksheet rather than where it was originally recorded.

Absolute Reference vs Relative Reference

The macro recorder uses absolute references by default, which means that Excel will store specific cell references as part of the code instructions. For example, if the macro was recorded in range A2:A5 in one worksheet, Excel will only perform the tasks in that range when you run the macro in any worksheet.

If you want a macro to perform the tasks in any range in a worksheet, enable the **Use Relative Reference** setting on the **View** or **Developer** tabs of the ribbon before recording the macro.

With the reference type set to relative, the macro will perform the actions relative to the active cell when the macro is run.

Recording a Macro

In the following example, we'll create reusable column and row headers. Once the process is recorded as a macro, we can run the macro whenever we want to insert those headers in a new worksheet.

The worksheet looks like this:

◢	A	B	C	D	E
1	**Sales**				
2					
3		New York	Los Angeles	London	Paris
4	Jan				
5	Feb				
6	Mar				
7	Apr				
8	May				
9	Jun				
10	Jul				
11	Aug				
12	Sep				
13	Oct				
14	Nov				
15	Dec				
16					

The process of creating the above template involves the following actions:

- Enter the text "Sales" in the first row. Set the font to bold and the font size to 14 points.

- Enter New York, Los Angeles, London, and Paris in cells B3 to E3.

- Select B3:E3, then Center and Bold the text.

- Increase the column width for B3:E3 to display all the text.

- Select B3:E3 and change the **Fill Color** to *Green, Accent 6, Lighter 40%*.

- Enter Jan to Dec in cells A4 to A15.

- Select A4:A15 and set the font to bold.

Follow the steps below to record the macro:

1. Open an Excel workbook and a blank worksheet. On the **View** tab, click the dropdown button of the **Macros** button (not the command button itself), then select **Use Relative References** from the menu.

2. On the **View** tab, click the dropdown button of the **Macros** button and click **Record Macro**. Excel opens the **Records Macro** dialog box.

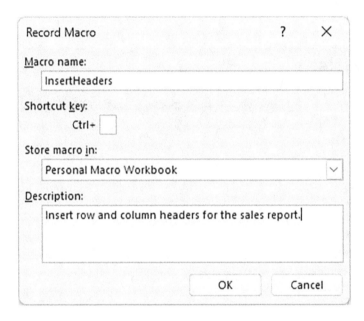

3. In the **Macro Name** field, enter the macro name. For example, *InsertHeaders*.

4. For the **Shortcut key**, hold down the **Shift** key and press **M**. This will enter Ctrl+Shift+M for the shortcut key. This keystroke can be used to run the macro. You can use other key combinations but avoid using popular Windows shortcut keys.

Note The shortcut key is optional, and you don't necessarily need to assign one to every macro you create.

---

5. In the **Store macro in** dropdown list, select **Personal Macro Workbook**. This ensures that the macro is saved in the global PERSONAL.XLSB workbook and not the current workbook.

6. In the **Description** box, enter a brief description of what the macro does. A description is optional but useful if you have a lot of macros. A brief description of each macro helps to differentiate between the macros and make maintenance easier.

7. Click **OK** to start recording.

    The Record Macro box is closed. On the status bar, next to Ready, you'll see a small square button indicating that the macro recorder is currently running.

    Next, we'll perform the Excel actions we'll be recording.

8. In cell A1, enter the text "Sales", then set the font to Bold and font size to 14 points.

9. Enter "New York", "Los Angeles", "London", and "Paris" in cells B3 to E3.

10. Select cells B3 to E3 and perform the following actions:

    - Set the column width to 12 (**Home** > **Cells** > **Format** > **Column Width**)
    - Set the text alignment to **Center**.
    - Set the font to **Bold**.
    - Change the **Fill Color** to *Green, Accent 6, Lighter 40%*.

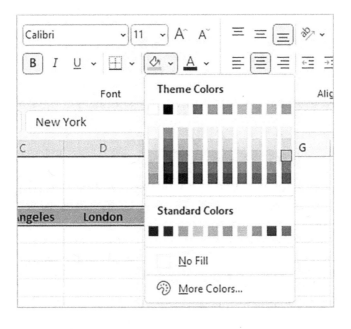

11. Enter "Jan" to "Dec" in cells A4 to A15.

12. Select cells A4 to A15 and set the font to Bold.

13. **Stop recording**: On the status bar, to the immediate right of **Ready**, you'll see a square button (the Record Macro/Stop Recording button). Click that button to stop recording the macro.

With that, your macro recording has been completed. Next, we'll run the macro.

Running a Macro

It is best to test a macro in a new worksheet (or a different range in the current worksheet) to see if the macro replicates actions you performed when recording it.

⚠️ **Important**

If you run a new macro in a worksheet with existing data, there is a risk that the macro will overwrite your existing data or formatting. Always test the macro in a new worksheet to ensure you don't mistakenly overwrite data. Only run the macro against production data when you're satisfied it is working as intended. For example, you may create a macro that adds formatting to existing data. In such cases, ensure you test the macro first against test copies of the data before running it against your production data.

To run a recorded macro, do the following:

1. Open the Macro dialog box.

    There are three ways you can open the **Macro** dialog box:

    -   On the **View** tab, in the **Macros** group, click the dropdown button on the **Macros** button and select **View Macros**.

    -   On the **Developer** tab, in the **Code** group, click the **Macros** button.

    -   Select **Alt+F8** on your keyboard to open the **Macro** dialog box.

    Excel opens the **Macro** dialog box, which lists all the macros you have created in the **Macro name** box.

2. To run a macro, select the macro name on the list and click the **Run** button.

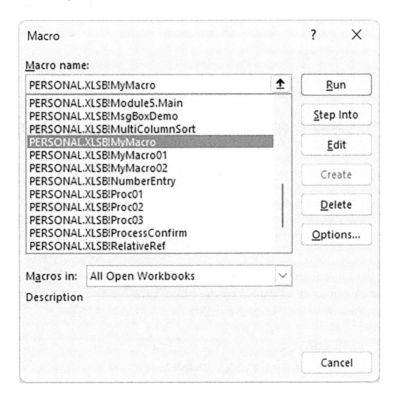

Tip If you assigned a keyboard shortcut to the macro, for example, Ctrl+Shift+M, you could use the keystroke to automatically run the macro without needing to open the Macro dialog box.

Add a Macro Button to the Ribbon

If you need to run your macro often, assigning it to a command button on the ribbon would be a good idea instead of running it from the Macros dialog box each time.

You must create a new custom group for your macro button, as you can't add the button to one of the default groups in Excel. You can create a new custom group in one of the default tabs and add your macro button. Alternatively, you can create a new custom tab to add your new custom group and a macro command button.

Create a New Custom Tab and Group

Follow the steps below to create a new tab and then add a command button to it:

1. To create a **new tab**, click the **New Tab** button at the bottom of the Main Tabs list box. Inside the tab, you must create at least one group before adding a command button from the left side of the dialog box.

2. To give the tab a display name, select the **New Tab (Custom)** item and click the **Rename** button at the bottom of the Main Tabs list box. Enter your preferred name for the tab in the **Rename** dialog box and click **OK**.

3. You can use the arrow buttons to the right of the Main Tabs list box to move your new tab item up or down the list, depending on where you want to place it.

4. To create a new **custom group**, select the tab where you want to create the group. This could be one of the default tabs or the new one you've created. Click **New**

Group (at the bottom of the dialog box). Excel creates a new group in the currently selected tab.

5. To create a name for the group, select the **New Group (Custom)** item and click the **Rename** button. Enter your preferred name in the **Rename** dialog box, for example, *MyMacros*.

6. Click **OK**.

You now have a custom group in which you can add your macro command buttons.

Assign A Macro Command to The New Group

Follow the steps below to add a macro command button to the new custom group:

1. Select your custom group in the **Main Tabs** list box.

2. Click the dropdown list box named **Choose commands from** (on the left of the dialog box) and select **Macros** from the dropdown list. In the list box on the left, you'll see a list of macros created in the current workbook and saved in the PERSONAL.XLSB workbook.

3. Select the macro name that you want to add to your custom group in the list box on the left, then click the **Add** button to add the macro command to the new custom group in the list box on the right.

Note If you mistakenly added the wrong command, select it in the list box on the right and click the **Remove** button to remove it.

4. Click **OK** on the Excel Options dialog box to confirm the change.

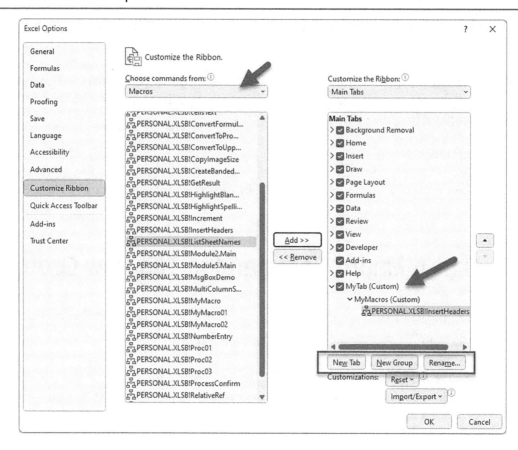

After adding the macro, the macro's name appears on a button with a generic icon (a program diagram chart). When you click the button, Excel runs the macro.

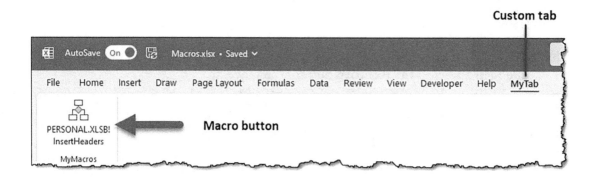

Assigning a Macro to a Button on the Quick Access Toolbar

You can also add a macro button to the Quick Access Toolbar if you have it displayed and use it regularly.

Follow the steps below to add a custom macro button to the Quick Access Toolbar:

1. Click the dropdown arrow at the end of the Quick Access toolbar.

2. On the dropdown menu, click **More Commands**.

    Excel displays the **Customize the Quick Access Toolbar** pane in Excel Options.

3. Select **Macros** from the dropdown list named **Choose commands from**.

    The list box below will display all macros created in the current workbook and those saved in the PERSONAL.XLSB workbook.

4. In the list box on the left, select the macro you want to add to the Quick Access Toolbar and click the **Add** button to add it to the list on the right.

    Note If you add the wrong command by mistake, select it in the list on the right and click the **Remove** button to remove it.

    ---

5. Click **OK**.

Excel displays your macro button as a generic macro icon on the Quick Access Toolbar. To run the macro, click the button.

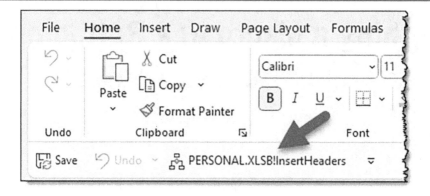

Assigning a Macro to an Image

You can assign macros to images you've inserted in your worksheet, including Pictures, Shapes, and Icons that you can insert from the **Illustrations** group on the **Insert** tab. You can also assign macros to images you have drawn using tools on the **Draw** tab.

To assign a macro to an image, do the following:

1. Insert the image in the worksheet area. For example, an icon from **Insert** > **Illustrations** > **Icons**.

2. Right-click the icon, and then click **Assign Macro** on its shortcut menu.

3. In the **Assign Macro** dialog box, select the macro name from the **Macro name** list box and click **OK**.

Now when you hover over the icon, the mouse pointer changes to a hand with a pointing index finger, indicating that you can click it to run the macro.

Assign a Macro to a Form Control Button

You can add an Excel **Form Control** from the Developer tab in your worksheet, which you can use to execute macros. The **Button Form Control** is like a button on a form to which you can assign a macro. When you click the button, the macro runs in the current worksheet.

To add a Button Form Control to your worksheet, do the following:

1. On the **Developer** tab, in the **Controls** group, click the **Insert** button. Then select the **Button** under **Form Controls**.

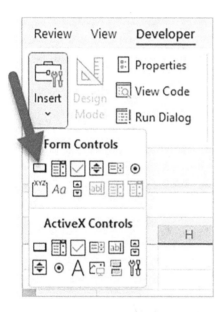

2. In the body of the worksheet, draw the button with your mouse.

3. As soon as you release the left mouse button, the **Assign Macro** dialog box will open. Select the macro you want to assign to the button from the Macro name box and click **OK**.

4. To edit the button's caption, right-click the button and select **Edit Text** on the shortcut menu, then type the caption you want for the button.

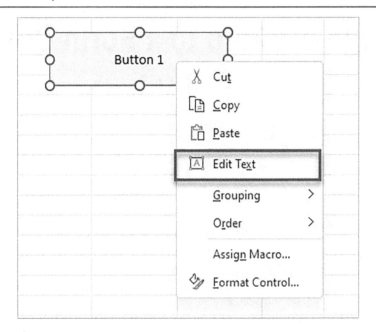

5. Click anywhere in the worksheet to exit the design mode. Excel deselects the button.

Your button is now set and ready for use. When you click the button, the macro assigned to it will run in the current worksheet.

Note When you right-click the button, the worksheet goes into design mode, and the button becomes inactive. To reactivate the button, click anywhere else in the worksheet. Excel deselects the button, and it responds to clicks again.

Formatting Controls

To format the button and change other properties, for example, the font or caption, right-click the button and select **Format Control** from the shortcut menu. Excel opens the **Format Control** dialog box, where you can change several control properties. When you're done, click **OK** on the Format Control dialog box. Then, click any cell in your worksheet to exit design mode.

Macro Security

Excel uses an authentication system called Microsoft Authenticode to digitally sign macro projects or add-ins created with Visual Basic for Applications. The macros you create locally on your computer are automatically authenticated. Hence, when you run them on your computer, Excel does not display a security alert.

For macros from an external source, the developer can acquire a certificate issued by a reputable authority or a trusted publisher. In such cases, Excel will run the macro if it can verify that it is from a trusted source.

If Excel cannot verify the digital signature of a macro from an external source because it perhaps doesn't have one, a security alert is displayed in the message bar (below the Excel ribbon). This alert allows you to enable the macro or ignore it. You can click the **Enable Content** button to run the macro if you trust the source and are sure that the macro poses no security threat to your computer.

If you try to create a macro in an Excel workbook that was saved as an XLSX file, Excel will display a message on the message bar prompting you to save the workbook as a macro-enabled file first. When you get this message, click the **Save As** button on the message bar, and select the **Excel Macro-Enabled Workbook (*.xlsm)** file type from the filter list.

File type	File extension
Excel Workbook	xlsx
Excel Macro-Enabled Workbook	xlsm

If you save the macro to the **Personal Macro Workbook**, it will be saved in the PERSONAL.XLSB file, which is an Excel Binary Workbook in the XLSTART folder. In this case, you'll not need to save your workbook as a macro-enabled workbook.

As much as possible, store macros in the **Personal Macro Workbook**. This means the macro is global to the computer and can be run from any workbook on the computer. It also means you don't need to convert your workbooks to macro-enabled files. Only create a macro-enabled workbook if it is necessary. For example, if you want to distribute the file to other people.

Trust Center Macro Settings

Microsoft Office security and privacy settings are located in the **Trust Center**. The Macro Settings tab of the Trust Center contains the macro security settings for your computer. Macro security is important to protect your computer against the threat of malicious code that can be inserted in Microsoft Office macros.

You can access the **Macro Settings** in the Trust Center in the following ways:

- On the **Developer** tab, in the **Code** group, click the **Macro Security** button. Excel opens the **Macro Settings** pane of the Trust Center dialog box.

- To go to macro settings, select **File** > **Options** > **Trust Center** > **Trust Centre Settings** > **Macro Settings**.

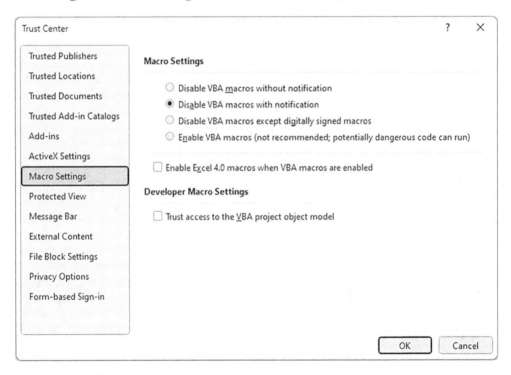

By default, Excel disables all macros from external sources with a security alert on the message bar, allowing you to enable the macro or ignore it. This setting is the default when you install Excel. However, there are other security options you can select.

You can also select one of these options in Macro Settings:

- **Disable all macros without notification**: This automatically disables macros in your computer. This setting means no macros will run on your computer, and you'll not get a security alert giving you the option to run the macro. This option is useful for shared computers, for instance, where you don't want anyone using the computer to run macros.

- **Disable all macros with notification**: This option is the default. All macros from external sources are disabled, with a security alert on the message bar. With this option, you have to specifically choose to enable the macro before it can run.

- **Disable all macros except digitally signed macros**: This option disables all macros apart from the digitally signed macros from publishers you have added to your **Trusted Publishers** in the Trust Center. With this option, a macro from a publisher not in your Trusted Publishers list will generate an alert with a message asking if you want to **Trust All Documents from this Publisher**. You can then choose to add them to your trusted publishers.

- **Enable all macros (not recommended; potentially dangerous code can run)**: This option enables all macros without any notifications or security alerts, even macros that are not digitally signed or authenticated. As indicated by the title, this option is not recommended because you can inadvertently run malicious code that corrupts your data or damages your computer.

Trusted Locations

The **Trusted Locations** tab of the Trust Center dialog box enables you to add, remove or modify trusted locations. If you are receiving macros from an external source that you need to run on your computer without alerts, then you need to place them in a trusted location on your computer. In doing so, Excel knows that these files are safe, and you are not prompted with security alerts when you open them.

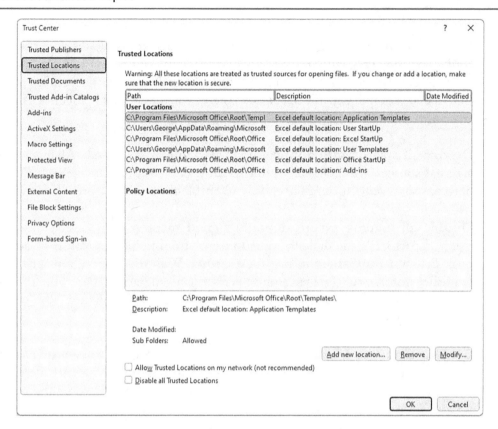

You can use the following options to change Trusted Locations settings:

- **Add new location**: To add a new trusted location, click the **Add new location** button at the bottom of the dialog box. On the **Microsoft Office Trusted Location** dialog box, click **Browse** and navigate to the folder you want to add to the list of trusted locations. After selecting the folder, click **OK** twice.

  Excel adds a new trusted location on your computer, and you can store any externally created macro-enabled files in that folder.

- **Allow trusted locations on my network (not recommended):** Select this option if you want to add folders on your network to your trusted locations. As indicated by the title, this is not recommended by Microsoft, as you can't entirely trust the safety of external locations. However, if you're working on a shared network drive that you trust and is the only way you can collaborate with others, this may be an option for sharing macro-enabled files. Only use it as a last option.

- **Disable all trusted locations**: Select this option if you want to immediately disable all trusted locations. With this option enabled, macros in your trusted locations will not run. Only the macros digitally signed and recognized as trustworthy by Excel will run on the computer.

Note The macro-enabled worksheets you create locally on your computer do not need to be stored in a trusted location to run on your computer. They're automatically digitally authenticated by Excel.

Editing Recorded Macros

As mentioned earlier in this chapter, the macros recorded in Excel are stored as Visual Basic for Applications (VBA) code instructions.

VBA programming is outside the scope of this book. However, knowing how to view the source code for your macro is useful, as you can identify and fix simple errors or make small changes to values. Sometimes, editing the macro in the Visual Basic Editor to change how it behaves is more expedient than recording it again.

Even if you have no programming skills, you may still be able to identify errors and make small changes. For example, you can fix spelling errors in the text, change number values, and correct formula errors. You don't need programming skills to make simple changes like these. You may also see something out of place in the code that helps you to avoid the error if you decide to re-record the macro.

Unhiding the Personal Macro Workbook

If the macro you want to edit is stored in your Personal Macro Workbook, you must unhide this workbook before you edit it in the Visual Basic Editor.

Follow the steps below to unhide the Personal Macro Workbook:

1. On the **View** tab, click the **Unhide** command button.

   Excel displays the **Unhide** dialog box showing the PERSONAL.XLSB workbook in the Unhide Workbook list.

2. Select PERSONAL.XLSB in the list box and click **OK** to unhide the workbook.

With the Personal Macro Workbook unhidden, you can edit macros saved in the Visual Basic Editor.

Editing the Macro in the Visual Basic Editor

Follow the steps below to open a macro for editing in the Visual Basic Editor:

1. Switch back to your main workbook.

2. On the **View** tab, click the **Macros** command button, then select **View Macros**.

   Excel opens the **Macro** dialog box listing the names of the macros created in the current workbook and the Personal Macro Workbook.

3. Select the macro you want to edit in the **Macro Name** box, and click the **Edit** button.

   Excel will display the macro in the Visual Basic Editor.

Project Explorer window   Code window

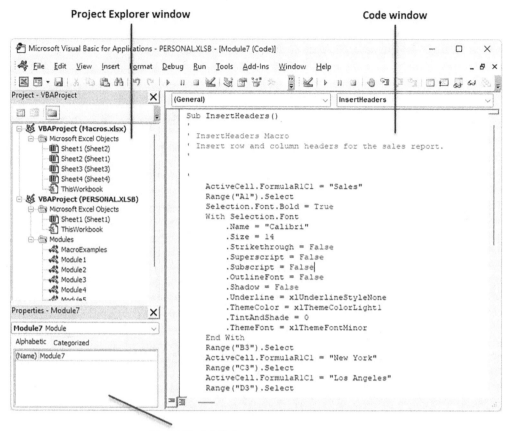

Properties window

The **Code window** shows the code instructions for the macro, and this is where you would edit the macro. The Project Explorer enables you to navigate to macros saved in different modules or workbooks currently open.

In the Code window, the macro code is between a starting keyword and an ending keyword. The beginning of the macro has the keyword **Sub InsertHeaders()** because **InsertHeaders** is the name given to the macro when it was created. The keyword **End Sub** indicates the end of the macro. To make changes to the macro, ensure you keep your edits within this area.

4. After making your changes, click the **Save** button on the Visual Basic Editor toolbar to save your changes (the blue disk icon).

5. Click the **Close** button to close the Visual Basic Editor. The close button is the x icon on the top right of the window. You can also close the window by selecting **File** > **Close and Return to Microsoft Excel**.

6. In the PERSONAL.XLSB workbook, select **View** tab > **Window** group > **Hide**.

   Hiding the file again prevents Excel from displaying the file when you next open Excel.

The code below was generated from the macro created earlier in this chapter.

```
Sub InsertHeaders()
'
' InsertHeaders Macro
' Insert row and column headers for the sales report.
'
    ActiveCell.FormulaR1C1 = "Sales"
    Range("A1").Select
    Selection.Font.Bold = True
    With Selection.Font
        .Name = "Calibri"
        .Size = 14
        .Strikethrough = False
        .Superscript = False
        .Subscript = False
        .OutlineFont = False
        .Shadow = False
        .Underline = xlUnderlineStyleNone
        .ThemeColor = xlThemeColorLight1
        .TintAndShade = 0
        .ThemeFont = xlThemeFontMinor
    End With
    Range("B3").Select
    ActiveCell.FormulaR1C1 = "New York"
    Range("C3").Select
    ActiveCell.FormulaR1C1 = "Los Angeles"
    Range("D3").Select
    ActiveCell.FormulaR1C1 = "London"
    Range("E3").Select
    ActiveCell.FormulaR1C1 = "Paris"
    Range("B3:E3").Select
```

```
    Selection.ColumnWidth = 12
    With Selection
        .HorizontalAlignment = xlCenter
        .VerticalAlignment = xlBottom
        .WrapText = False
        .Orientation = 0
        .AddIndent = False
        .IndentLevel = 0
        .ShrinkToFit = False
        .ReadingOrder = xlContext
        .MergeCells = False
    End With
    Selection.Font.Bold = True
    With Selection.Interior
        .Pattern = xlSolid
        .PatternColorIndex = xlAutomatic
        .ThemeColor = xlThemeColorAccent6
        .TintAndShade = 0.399975585192419
        .PatternTintAndShade = 0
    End With
    Range("A4").Select
    ActiveCell.FormulaR1C1 = "Jan"
    Range("A4").Select
    Selection.AutoFill Destination:=Range("A4:A15"),
Type:=xlFillDefault
    Range("A4:A15").Select
    Selection.Font.Bold = True
    Range("B4").Select
End Sub
```

Chapter 7

Analyze Alternative Data Sets with What-If Analysis

This chapter covers the following:

- What-If Analysis for one-variable and two-variable data tables.

- Using the Scenario Manager to create and compare different scenarios for your data.

- Using the Goal Seek tool to adjust variables in a data set to meet a goal.

- Using the Solver add-in tool to generate alternate scenarios for more complex data.

Spreadsheet formulas are excellent at automatically updating results based on your input. For that reason, spreadsheets are one of the best tools for carrying out financial projections based on assumptions. Excel provides a whole raft of tools for just this purpose.

In Excel, there are different types of What-If Analysis you can perform. In this chapter, we will cover four commonly used types in Excel.

- **Data tables**: This feature enables you to generate a series of projections based on one or two changing variables.

- **Goal seeking**: This feature enables you to set a predetermined goal and then choose the variables that will change to meet this goal.

- **Scenarios**: In this type of What-If Analysis, you create different scenarios using alternative figures, which you can compare side-by-side in a generated report.

- **Solver**: The Solver is an Excel add-in that you can use to create more complex What-If Analysis, enabling you to use multiple variables and constraints.

Data Tables

A data table gives you a projection of how your bottom line would look if one or two variables in your data were changed. For example, what would be our profit if we achieved a growth rate in sales of 1.5% rather than 1%? What would be our net profit next year if we reduced our expenses by 3%? These are the kinds of questions that a data table can answer.

Creating a One-Variable Data Table

The one-variable data table is a projection based on a series of values you want to substitute for a single input value. To demonstrate this data table, we will use an example where we create a series of projected sales for the next quarter.

In this example, we have the following figures:

- Sales for quarter one: $45,000.
- Projected growth in sales for quarter two: 2.0%.
- Projected sales for quarter two: 45,000 + (45,000 x 0.02).

For this projection, we want to substitute different growth rates into the projected growth for Qtr 2 to see a series of projected sales based on different growth rates.

For the column values, we enter rates ranging from 1% to 5% in range B8:B16, with an increment of 0.5%. You can use different increments based on your requirements.

For the row value, cell **C8**, we enter *=B5,* which is a reference to the master formula which calculates **Projected Sales Qtr 2**. The data table will use this master formula as the base figure to make the projections.

B5			✗ ✓	fx	=B3+(B3*B4)	

◢	A	B	C	D
1	**Projected sales for Quarter 2 - one-variable data table**			
2				
3	Sales Qtr 1	$45,000.00		
4	Growth Qtr 2	2.00%		
5	Projected Sales Qtr 2	$45,900.00		
6				
7			$45,900.00	
8		1.00%		
9		1.50%		
10		2.00%		
11		2.50%		
12		3.00%		
13		3.50%		
14		4.00%		
15		4.50%		
16		5.00%		
17				
18	B8:B16 = Growth rates			
19	C7 = Master formula			
20				

Once your data has been prepared, as shown above, follow the steps below to generate the data table:

1. Select the table. For this example, it is B7:C16.

2. On the **Data** tab, in the **Forecast** group, select **What-If Analysis > Data Table**.

   Excel displays the **Data Table** dialog box.

3. Click in the **Column input cell** box, and on the worksheet, select the growth percentage, cell **B4**. This example is a one-variable data table, so we only need the column input.

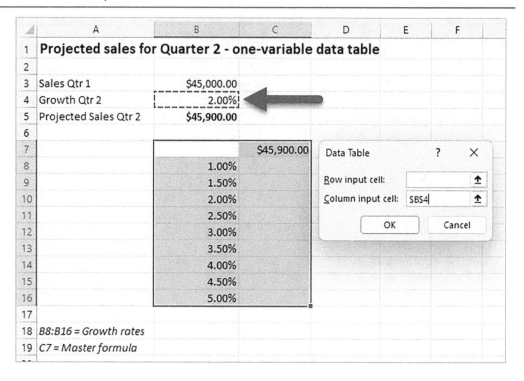

4. Click **OK** to generate the projected sale values in cells C8:C16.

| C8 | | | | fx | {=TABLE(,B4)} | | |

◢	A	B	C	D	E	F	G
1	Projected sales for Quarter 2 - one-variable data table						
2							
3	Sales Qtr 1	$45,000.00					
4	Growth Qtr 2	2.00%					
5	Projected Sales Qtr 2	$45,900.00					
6							
7			$45,900.00		B8:B16 = Growth rates		
8		1.00%	$45,450.00		C7 = Master formula		
9		1.50%	$45,675.00		C8:C16 = Projected sales		
10		2.00%	$45,900.00				
11		2.50%	$46,125.00				
12		3.00%	$46,350.00				
13		3.50%	$46,575.00				
14		4.00%	$46,800.00				
15		4.50%	$47,025.00				
16		5.00%	$47,250.00				

The data table is created as an array formula using the TABLE function. The TABLE function takes two arguments *row_ref* and/or *column_ref*, but only needs one for a one-variable data table.

{=TABLE(,B4)}

The formula shows that the value in cell B4 represents its *column_ref* argument for which alternate values are provided in cells B8:B16. The process simply substitutes the original rate in B4 with the series of rates in B8:B16 to generate the projected values.

As the data table uses an array formula, Excel will not allow you to delete only some of the values in the array. To delete values in the data table, you must select all the generated values, cells C8:C16, and select the **Delete** key.

Creating a Two-Variable Data Table

A two-variable data table enables you to create projections based on the changing values of two variables.

Creating a two-variable table is similar to the one-variable data table described above. But, in this case, we have two variables that can change instead of one. A two-variable data table requires input for the column and row fields, so we need a series of values for the table's first column and first row. At the intersection of the row and column, we enter the master formula, which would have the figure we want to use as the basis of the projection.

To demonstrate this type of data table, we will use an example where we create a series of projected sales for the next quarter based on two variables.

In this example, we have the following figures:
- Sales for quarter one: $45,000.
- Projected growth in sales for quarter two: 2.0%.
- Expenses for quarter two: 15%.
- Projected sales for quarter two: 45,000 + (45,000*0.02).

We want to see a projection of our sales with different growth rates (between 1% and 5%) and expense rates (between 15% and 30%).

| B6 | | | fx | =B3+(B3*B4)-(B3*B5) | | |

◢	A	B	C	D	E	F
1	**Projection on sales - two-variable data table**					
2						
3	Sales Qtr 1	$45,000.00				
4	Growth Qtr 2	1.80%				
5	Expenses Qtr 2	15%				
6	Projected Sales Qtr 2	£39,060.00				
7						
8		£39,060.00	15%	20%	25%	30%
9		1.00%				
10		1.50%				
11		2.00%				
12		2.50%				
13		3.00%				
14		3.50%				
15		4.00%				
16		4.50%				
17		5.00%				
18						
19	*B9:B17 = Growth rates, B8 = Master formula, C8:F8 = Expenses*					

For the row entries we want to substitute in **Expenses Qtr 2**, we enter values ranging from 15% to 30% in cells C8:F8.

For the column entries we want to substitute in **Growth Qtr 2**, we enter values ranging from 1% to 5% (increasing by 0.5%) in cells B9:B17.

In cell B8, we enter *=B6*, a reference to the master formula that calculates **Projected Sales Qtr 2**.

As shown in the image above, with the worksheet model prepared, follow the steps below to generate the data table:

1. Select the table. For this example, the range is B8:F17.

2. On the **Data** tab, in the **Forecast** group, select **What-If Analysis > Data Table**.

   Excel displays the **Data Table** dialog box.

We must enter both input values in the Data Table dialog because this is a two-variable data table.

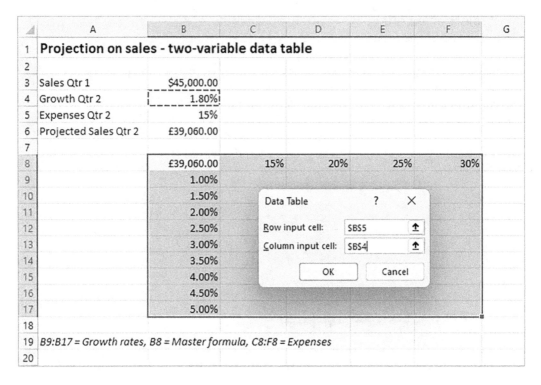

3. Click in the **Row input cell** box, and on the worksheet, select the expenses for quarter two, cell **B5**.

4. Next, click in the **Column input cell** box, and then on the worksheet, select the growth percentage, cell **B4**.

5. Click **OK** to generate the projected values in the data table.

| C9 | | ▾ | : | ✕ | ✓ | *fx* | {=TABLE(B5,B4)} | | |

◢	A	B	C	D	E	F	G
1	**Projection on sales - two-variable data table**						
2							
3	Sales Qtr 1	$45,000.00					
4	Growth Qtr 2	1.80%					
5	Expenses Qtr 2	15%					
6	Projected Sales Qtr 2	£39,060.00					
7							
8		£39,060.00	15%	20%	25%	30%	
9		1.00%	£38,700.00	£36,450.00	£34,200.00	£31,950.00	
10		1.50%	£38,925.00	£36,675.00	£34,425.00	£32,175.00	
11		2.00%	£39,150.00	£36,900.00	£34,650.00	£32,400.00	
12		2.50%	£39,375.00	£37,125.00	£34,875.00	£32,625.00	
13		3.00%	£39,600.00	£37,350.00	£35,100.00	£32,850.00	
14		3.50%	£39,825.00	£37,575.00	£35,325.00	£33,075.00	
15		4.00%	£40,050.00	£37,800.00	£35,550.00	£33,300.00	
16		4.50%	£40,275.00	£38,025.00	£35,775.00	£33,525.00	
17		5.00%	£40,500.00	£38,250.00	£36,000.00	£33,750.00	
18							
19	B9:B17 = Growth rates, B8 = Master formula, C8:F8 = Expenses, C9:F17 = Projected sales						
20							

The two-variable data table uses the TABLE function to create an array formula in the output range of C9:F17. The TABLE function takes two arguments *row_ref* and/or *column_ref*.

{=TABLE(B5,B4)}

The formula shows that cell B5 is the *row_ref* argument for which alternate values have been provided in cells C8:F8. The *column_ref* argument has cell B4, for which there are alternate values in cells B9:B17.

The process substitutes the original values with those in B9:B17 and C8:F8 to generate the projection.

As the data table uses an array formula, you can't delete only some of the values in the array. To delete the generated data in the table, select all values in cells C9:F17 and select the **Delete** key.

Scenario Manager

Another tool provided by Excel that you can use to create a What-If Analysis is the Scenario Manager. The Scenario Manager enables you to create different scenarios where certain input values are changed to produce different results.

You can assign names to the different scenarios in the scenario manager. For example, *Most Likely*, *Best Case*, and *Worst Case*. Once you've created the scenarios in the Scenario Manager, you can view the different scenarios in your worksheet. You can also generate a summary report with all the scenarios to compare them side-by-side.

Adding Scenarios

In the following example, we will create projections for the next year based on figures from the current year. The scenarios will apply different growth rates to the current figures so that we can compare the scenarios together in a summary report.

Figures – Current Year
- Sales: $627,198.00
- Cost of production: $200,000
- Office supplies: $5,000
- Vehicle: $10,500.00
- Building: $50,000.00

| C4 | ⌄ : ✕ ✓ fx | =B4+(B4*D4) | |

◢	A	B	C	D
1	**Projection Scenarios**			
2				
3		Current	Projected	Growth assumptions
4	Sales	$627,198.00	$639,741.96	2.00%
5	Cost of production	($200,000.00)	($203,000.00)	1.50%
6	Office supplies	($5,000.00)	($5,075.00)	1.50%
7	Vehicle	($10,500.00)	($10,657.50)	1.50%
8	Building	($50,000.00)	($50,750.00)	1.50%
9	Profit	$361,698.00	$370,259.46	
10				

The projected value in C4 is calculated with the following formula:

=B4+(B4*D4)

The formula under **Projected** increments the current value by the growth assumption (percentage rate). The same formula is used to derive the values in cells C5:C8.

We want to create more scenarios using different growth assumptions without overwriting the original data, as we want to compare multiple scenarios. The Scenario Manager comes in handy for scenarios like this.

-🔆-**Tip**
When using the Scenario Manager, it is a good idea to name each cell you intend to change. It makes it easier to know what each cell represents when you enter the new values in a subsequent dialog box. It also makes your subsequent reports of the scenarios easier to understand. Named Ranges are covered in my *Excel 2022 Basics* book.

Follow the steps below to create different scenarios with the Scenario Manager:

1. Select the changing cells in the worksheet. In this case, the changing cells are D4:D8.

2. On the **Data** tab, in the **Forecast** group, select **What-If Analysis > Scenario Manager**.

   Excel opens the **Scenario Manager** dialog box.

3. Click the **Add** button to add a new scenario.

4. Enter a name for the scenario in the **Scenario name** field. These can be names like *Most likely, Best case, Worst case,* etc.

5. The **Changing cells** box should already have the reference to the cells you selected before opening the Scenario Manager dialog box. However, if the right cells have not been selected, click the Expand Dialog button on the field (up arrow) and select the cells in the worksheet.

6. The **Comment** box is optional. You can enter a short description for the scenario or leave the default text, a log of when it was last updated.

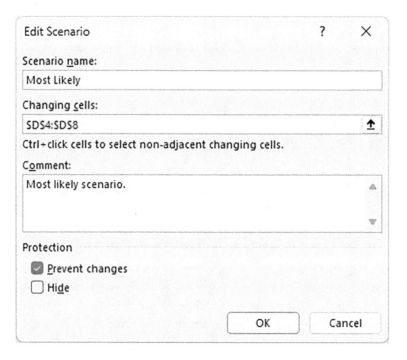

7. In the **Protection** portion of the screen, accept the default selection for the **Prevent changes** checkbox. This setting means Excel protects the scenario from changes when worksheet protection is turned on. If you don't want to protect the scenario when the worksheet is protected, uncheck Prevent changes.

8. Leave the **Hide** checkbox unselected if you don't want the scenario hidden when worksheet protection is on. Alternatively, select the Hide checkbox if you want Excel to hide the scenario when the worksheet is protected.

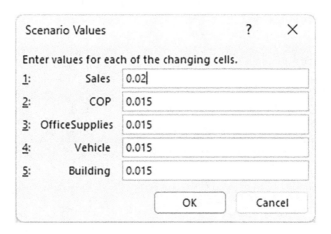 **Note** Worksheet protection is a separate topic not related to What-If Analysis and is covered elsewhere in this book.

9. Click **OK** to open the **Scenario Values** dialog box.

Scenario Values	?	X

Enter values for each of the changing cells.

<u>1</u>:	Sales	0.02|
<u>2</u>:	COP	0.015
<u>3</u>:	OfficeSupplies	0.015
<u>4</u>:	Vehicle	0.015
<u>5</u>:	Building	0.015

OK	Cancel

10. The Scenario Values dialog box contains several boxes for the changing cells. As shown in the image above, naming the changing cells becomes useful here as each box is labeled with a cell name rather than a cell reference.

    For the first scenario, you may want to accept the values already in the text box (if you had values in the cells before starting the Scenario Manager). If you want a different set of values for your first scenario, you can change them here.

11. When done, click the **Add** button to save the scenario and return to the **Add Scenario** dialog box.

12. Repeat steps **4** to **11** above to add the other scenarios you want to create.

13. When you're done, close the Scenario Values dialog box and return to the Scenario Manager.

Viewing and Editing Scenarios

1. Open the Scenario Manager dialog box if it's not already open (**Data** > **Forecast** >**What-If Analysis** > **Scenario Manager**).

   In the Scenario Manager dialog box, you'll see the names of all the scenarios you've added under **Scenarios**.

2. To view a scenario, select its name under **Scenarios** and click the **Show** button.

   You can also double-click a scenario name to view it in the worksheet. For example, double-click *Best Case* in the **Scenarios** box to display the *Best Case* scenario.

   Excel closes the Scenario Manager dialog box and inserts the rates entered for the *Best Case* scenario in our table.

3. To delete a scenario, select it and click **Delete**. Excel removes that scenario from the Scenario Manager.

4. To edit a scenario, select the scenario under **Scenarios** and click **Edit**. Excel takes you through the editing process, where you can change the name of the scenario, the changing cells, and the values for the cells. If you only want to change the values, click through to the **Scenario Values** dialog box and change the values there.

Merging Scenarios

The Scenario Manager dialog box also enables you to merge scenarios from other Excel workbooks that are open. Note that the workbooks must share the same data layout and changing cells for you to merge their scenarios.

To merge scenarios from another workbook, do the following:

1. Click the **Merge** button in the Scenario Manager dialog box. Excel displays the **Merge Scenarios** dialog box.

2. Select the workbook name from the **Book** dropdown list box.

3. In the **Sheet** box, select the worksheet and then click **OK**.

All the scenarios in that worksheet are then copied and merged with the current worksheet.

Summary Reports

After creating the different scenarios, you can compare them in a summary report.

To generate a summary report for the scenarios you have entered:

1. In the **Scenario Manager** dialog box, click the **Summary** button.

   Excel opens the **Scenario Summary** dialog box.

2. Select **Report type** if it is not already selected.

3. Click the **Results cells** text box and select the result cells in your worksheet. These would be the cells with the totals for your projection. For our example, our **Profit** cell is C9.

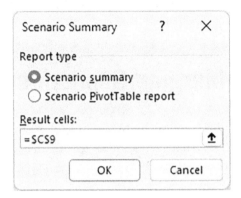

4. Click **OK** to generate the report.

Excel will generate a report in a separate worksheet showing all the scenarios you have created.

Scenario Summary				
	Current Values:	Most Likely	Best Case	Worst Case
Changing Cells:				
Sales	2.00%	2.00%	5.00%	1.00%
COP	1.50%	1.50%	1.00%	8.00%
OfficeSupplies	1.50%	1.50%	1.00%	2.50%
Vehicle	1.50%	1.50%	1.00%	5.00%
Building	1.50%	1.50%	1.20%	5.00%
Result Cells:				
Profit	$370,259.46	$370,259.46	$390,302.90	$348,819.98

Notes: Current Values column represents values of changing cells at time Scenario Summary Report was created. Changing cells for each scenario are highlighted in gray.

As you can see from the image above, assigning names to the changing cells and result cells in your worksheet comes in handy when generating a scenario summary.

You may wonder why we need to use the scenario manager when we could have just entered the different scenarios directly in the Excel worksheet area. The example used here with the scenario manager is simple for demonstration purposes only. However, the scenario manager comes in handy when the complexity of the data model makes it difficult to enter the different scenarios side-by-side in Excel in a meaningful way.

Goal Seeking

On some occasions, when working with data in Excel, you already have the outcome you want to achieve in mind, and you would like to know the various input values that will achieve that outcome or goal. For example, you may have a goal of $600,000 in revenue, and to achieve that goal, you need a certain amount for your sales against the cost of expenses. This kind of scenario is where the Goal Seek feature in Excel comes in handy.

The **Goal Seek** command in Excel enables you to set a goal in one cell and then choose the cell whose value you would like Excel to adjust in other to meet your goal. So, this is like working backward, stating the results first and allowing Goal Seek to determine the inputs needed to meet that goal. The goal cell will have a formula based on the input from other cells, including the cell that Excel will change.

For example, let's say we want to find how much sales we need to generate to reach a certain income level. Instead of making several adjustments to the sales figure to produce the desired result, we can simply set the desired result and let Goal Seek work out the sales figure required to achieve the result.

Example

To demonstrate the Goal Seek feature in Excel, we'll use an example to forecast the income based on a range of input values.

	A	B	C
1	**Income Forecast for 2024**		
2			
3			
4	Sales	$600,250.00	
5	Cost of production	($139,705.00)	
6	Gross Profit	$460,545.00	
7	Expenses	($84,267.00)	
8	Income	$376,278.00	
9			

In the table above, cell **B8** has a formula that calculates the *Income*, which is the sum of the *Gross Profit* and the *Expenses* (this is a negative value as indicated by brackets).

=B6+B7

Our goal-seeking question is:

What amount should our sales be if we want to generate an income of $500,000?

Once the figures have been entered in the worksheet, follow the steps below to perform the goal-seeking:

1. On the **Data** tab, in the **Forecast** group, select **What-If Analysis > Goal Seek**.

    Excel displays the **Goal Seek** dialog box.

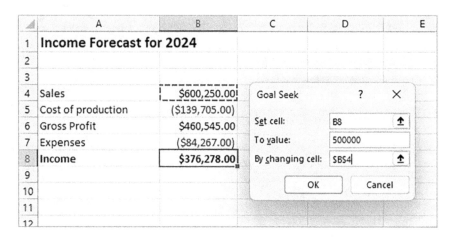

2. Click in the **Set cell** box and select the cell in the worksheet that contains the formula that will return the value you're seeking. For our example, this is cell **B8**.

3. In the **To value** box, enter the goal value. For our example, the value will be 500,000.

4. Click in the **By changing cell** box and select the cell that contains the value you want Excel to adjust to achieve the goal. For this example, this will be cell **B4**.

5. Click **OK**.

Excel displays the **Goal Seek Status** dialog box, which informs you that a solution has been found and that the result value is now the same as the target value.

◢	A	B	C	D	E
1	Income Forecast for 2024				
2					
3					
4	Sales	$723,972.00			
5	Cost of production	($139,705.00)			
6	Gross Profit	$584,267.00			
7	Expenses	($84,267.00)			
8	Income	$500,000.00			
9					
10					
11					
12					

Goal Seek Status ? ×

Goal Seeking with Cell B8 found a solution.   Step

Target value: 500000   Pause
Current value: $500,000.00

OK   Cancel

If the Goal Seek does not find a solution, it will enable the **Step** and **Pause** buttons to enable you to step through different options to find a solution.

6. Click **OK** to accept this result, or click **Cancel** if you don't want to keep the result.

Excel will overwrite your existing values if you click OK to accept the value.

If you want to return to the previous values, you can undo the change by clicking the **Undo** button on the **Home** tab or selecting Ctrl+Z on your keyboard.

To switch back and forth between the previous value and the new value returned by Goal Seek, use the **Undo** and **Redo** buttons on the Home tab. Alternatively, you can select Ctrl+Z to display the original values and Ctrl+Y to display the Goal Seek values.

Using The Solver for Complex Problems

The Data Table and Goal Seek commands are great for creating What-If Analysis solutions for simpler problems requiring a direct relationship between the inputs and the outputs. However, for more complex problems, Excel provides another tool, which is the **Solver** add-in utility.

The Solver can be used when you create a solution that requires changing multiple input values in your model. The Solver also enables you to impose constraints on the input and output values.

The Solver uses an iterative method to find the optimum solution based on the inputs, the desired result, and the constraints you have set.

Complex problems can have different ways they're solved, and the Solver tries to present the best solution for you. Sometimes, the solution returned may not be the best for your situation. For example, suppose several variables need to be changed. In that case, the Solver may produce a combination of figures that may not suit your specific needs (even if the result meets the objective). Hence, you may want to run the Solver multiple times to get the best solution.

To set up the problem in the Solver, you will need to define the following items:

- **Objective cell**: The target cell that you can set to maximum, minimum, or a specific value. The objective cell needs to be a formula.

- **Variable cells**: These are the changing cells in your worksheet. The Goal Seek method, for example, enables you to only specify one cell that can be changed. The difference with the Solver is that you can have multiple cells that can be changed to achieve the objective.

- **Constraints**: The cells containing the values you want to use to set a limit or restriction to the range of changes that can be made. For instance, you could set a constraint that says the *Sales* figure cannot be increased by more than 10% to achieve the solution (perhaps because a sales figure of more than 10% would be unrealistic for this particular problem).

After setting the parameters in the Solver, Excel returns the optimum solution by changing the values in your worksheet. At this point, you can retain the changes in your worksheet or restore your original values. The Solver also enables you to save the solution as a scenario you can view later.

The Solver can be used with the Scenario Manager to set up a problem to solve. The variable cells you define when you use the Scenario Manager to set up a scenario are available and picked up by the Solver. The Solver also allows you to save solutions as scenarios which will then be available to the Scenario Manager.

Enabling the Solver Add-in

The Solver is an add-in and may not be available on your ribbon if it hasn't been manually added, as it is not added by the default Excel installation.

Follow the steps below to add the Solver command button to your Excel ribbon:

1. Select **File** > **Options** > **Add-ins**.
2. At the bottom of the Add-ins tab, ensure that the **Manage** dropdown list has **Excel Add-ins** selected.
3. Click **Go**.
4. Select the **Solver Add-in** option in the **Add-ins** dialog and click **OK**.

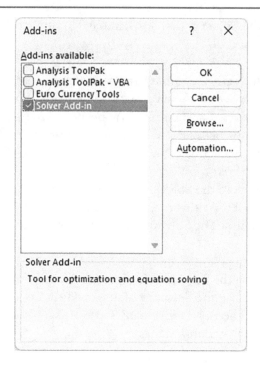

The **Solver** command button can be found on the **Data** tab in the **Analyze** group.

Solver Example

In the following example, we will use the Solver to find a solution to what combination of figures can generate an income of $680,500.00. The worksheet model created for the problem is shown below.

C4		∨ : ✕ ✓ fx	=$B$4+($B$4*SalesGrowth)	

◢	A	B	C	D
1	**Sales Forecast**			
2				
3		Qtr 1	Qtr 2	Assumptions
4	Sales	$800,250.40	$840,262.92	5%
5	Cost of production	($139,705.00)	($148,087.30)	6%
6	Gross Profit	$660,545.40	$692,175.62	
7	Expenses	($84,267.00)	($90,165.69)	7%
8	Income	$576,278.40	$602,009.93	
9				

The value in C4 is calculated with the following formula:

=$B$4+($B$4*SalesGrowth)

SalesGrowth is the name given to cell **D4**, which is currently 5%. The formulas in the **Qtr 2** column simply increment the **Qtr 1** values by the growth rates under **Assumptions**.

For this example, the changing/variable cells will be those in the Assumptions column, while the result/objective cell will be **C8** (which is named **Income_Qtr2**).

Once you have loaded the Solver add-in and created your worksheet model, follow the steps below to define a problem with the Solver:

1. On the **Data** tab, in the **Analyze** group, click the **Solver** command button.

   Excel opens the **Solver Parameters** dialog box.

2. In the **Solver Parameters** dialog box, the **Set Objective** box is the result you want to achieve. Enter a reference to a cell on the worksheet with a formula. Click in the **Set Objective** box and select the cell on your worksheet.

   For our example, this is cell **C8** on the worksheet. The name of the cell is **Income_Qtr2**, so the name is inserted in the text box.

3. You can set the Objective to the following options:

   ▪ **Max**: As large as possible based on the input values available.

- **Min**: As small as possible.
- **Value Of**: A specific value.

For this example, we are using a specific value for our objective. Select **Value Of** and enter 680500.

4. Click the **By Changing Variable Cells** text box and select the cells you want to change in the worksheet.

   To select non-adjacent cells, hold down the **Ctrl** key while clicking the cells. Excel will enter cell names in place of cell references if they have been named.

5. In the **Subject to the Constraints** box, you can add constraints to limit the changes the Solver can make. To add a constraint, click the **Add** button.

   Excel displays the **Add Constraint** dialog box.

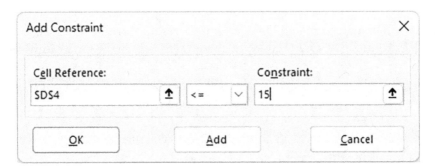

6. In the **Add Constraints** dialog box, click in the **Cell Reference** box, then select the cell on the worksheet for which you want to create a constraint.

   Select the relationship from the dropdown list box in the middle. The options are =, <=, >=, int (for integer), and bin (for binary). For our example, we select <= from the dropdown list.

   In the **Constraint** box, enter the constraint. For this example, we don't want the *SalesGrowth* to be more than 15%, so we enter 15%.

   Click **Add** to insert the constraint and continue adding more constraints (or click **OK** to return to the Solver Parameters dialog box if you're done).

   The constraint you added will now be listed in the **Subject to the Constraints** box.

7. For our example, we'll leave the **Make Unconstrained Variables Non-Negative** checkbox selected, which is the default. Clear this checkbox if you want to allow negative values in variable cells for which you've set no constraints.

8. The default value for the **Select a Solving Method** dropdown list will have the default value is **GRG Nonlinear**.

   There are three solving methods:

   - **GRG Nonlinear** is for solving smooth nonlinear problems.

   - **Simplex LP** method is for linear problems.

   - **Evolutionary** method is for non-smooth problems.

   Accept the GRG Nonlinear default, unless you're sure one of the other methods is more optimal for your problem. Excel displays a brief description of the solving methods in the label below the dropdown list box.

9. After entering all the parameters in the Solver Parameters dialog box, click the **Solve** button.

Solver Results

When you click **Solve** on the Solver Parameters dialog box, the box will disappear. Depending on your problem's complexity, you may see an indicator on Excel's status bar informing you of the progress of the Solver. On most occasions, however, the solution would be generated quickly, and Excel will display the **Solver Results** dialog box.

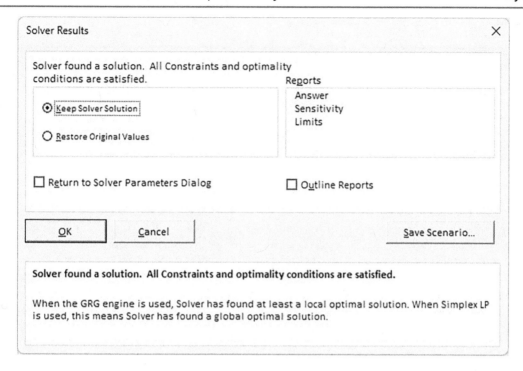

The **Solver Results** dialog box informs you whether a solution was found for your problem. If a solution is not found, the dialog box will inform you that a solution cannot be found, and you will have the opportunity to go back and adjust the parameters.

The Solver will display the new values in your worksheet if a solution is found. However, the Solver Results dialog box will allow you to keep the values provided by the solution or restore your original values.

To keep the solution, select **Keep Solver Solution** (if it is not already selected), and click **OK**.

◢	A	B	C	D	E
1	**Sales Forecast**				
2					
3		**Qtr 1**	**Qtr 2**	**Assumptions**	
4	Sales	$800,250.40	$915,620.72	14%	
5	Cost of production	($139,705.00)	($145,790.62)	4%	
6	Gross Profit	$660,545.40	$769,830.10		
7	Expenses	($84,267.00)	($89,330.10)	6%	
8	Income	$576,278.40	$680,500.00		
9					
10					
11					
12					

From the worksheet model in the image above, you can see that the Solver changed the growth percentages for *Sales* (14%), *Cost of Production* (4%), and *Expenses* (6%) to achieve the target *Income* for *Qtr 2* of $680,500.00. You may also notice that the Solver stayed within the 15% constraint set for the *SalesGrowth* cell.

Select **Restore Original Values** if you do not want to keep the solution and instead return to the original values in your worksheet.

To save the solution as a scenario before restoring your original values, click the **Save Scenario** button and assign a name to it. Once you have saved it, you can select the Restore Original Values option and click **OK** to close the Solver Results dialog box.

You can also click the **Cancel** button on the Solver Results dialog box to dismiss the Solver and return your original values.

Note If you keep the solution provided by the Solver, unlike the Goal Seek command, you can't undo the changes by clicking the Undo command on the Quick Access Toolbar. If you want to retain your original values, select **Restore Original Values,** and then click **Save Scenario** to save the scenario for later viewing. That way, you can keep your original values in the worksheet and use the Scenario Manager (covered previously in this chapter) to display the solution generated by the Solver.

Solver Options

The default options used by the Solver are adequate for most problems. However, for some scenarios, you may want to change the options before generating a solution with the Solver.

To change the Solver options, click the **Options** button in the Solver Parameters dialog box.

Excel opens the **Options** dialog box with three tabs: All Methods, GRG Nonlinear, and Evolutionary.

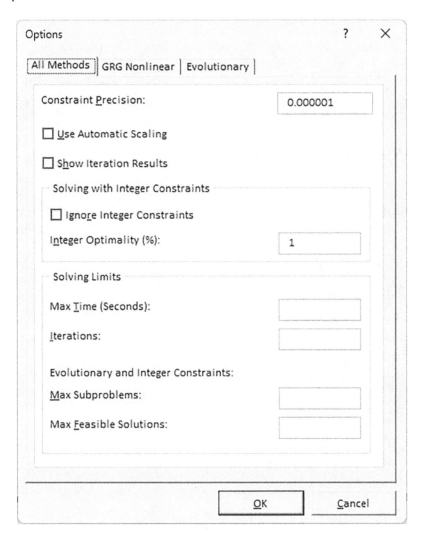

The following settings apply to the Solver options.

- **Constraint Precision**: This specifies the precision of the constraints added. To satisfy a constraint, the relationship between the cell reference and the value of the constraint cannot be more than this amount. The smaller this number is, the higher the precision.

- **Use Automatic Scaling**: Select this option if you want the Solver to automatically scale the results.

- **Show Iteration Results**: Select this option if you want the Solver to show the results for the iterations it followed in solving the problem.

- **Ignore Integer Constraints**: Select this checkbox if you want the Solver to ignore any specified constraints that use integers.

- **Integer Optimality (%)**: This option specifies the percentage of Integer Optimality the Solver applies when solving the problem.

- **Max Time (Seconds)**: Specifies the maximum number of seconds that you want the Solver to spend in finding a solution before it times out.

- **Iterations**: This value specifies the maximum number of iterations you want the Solver to make in recalculating the worksheet when finding the solution.

- **Max Subproblems**: Specifies the maximum number of subproblems you want the Solver to take when using the Evolutionary method to solve the problem.

- **Max Feasible Solutions**: This value specifies the maximum number of feasible solutions you want the Solver to pursue when using the Evolutionary method to solve the problem.

Note that the Options dialog box also has the **GRG Nonlinear** and **Evolutionary** tabs where you can make additional changes to the settings.

After making changes to the Solver options, click **OK** to return to the Solver Parameters dialog box.

Tip Only change to an option in the Solver if you understand what that setting represents and how the change will affect your worksheet model. Otherwise, the default values will suffice for most Solver problems.

Saving Solver Problem Models

When you save your workbook, the objective cell, variable cells, constraint, and Solver options that were last entered in the Solver Parameters dialog box are saved as part of the worksheet. These parameters will be loaded in the Solver Parameters dialog box the next time it is opened.

When you create other problem models for the worksheet you want to save, you must use the **Load/Save** button in the **Solver Parameters** dialog box to save them.

To save an additional Solver model, do the following:

1. In the **Solver Parameters** dialog box, click the **Load/Save** button.

   Excel displays the **Load/Save Model** dialog box.

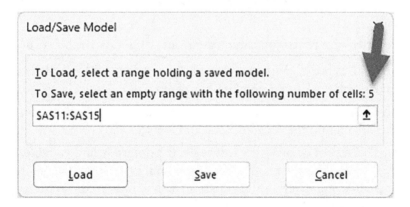

2. On the **Load/Save** dialog, click in the text box and select an empty vertical range in your worksheet with enough cells to hold all the parameters you entered for the problem model. The text above in the text box will tell you how many cells you need to select.

3. Click **Save** after entering the range in the text box.

    Excel saves the values to that range in your worksheet.

Loading a Saved Solver Model

To load a saved Solver model, do the following:

1. In the **Solver Parameters** dialog box, click the **Load/Save** button.

    Excel displays the **Load/Save Model** dialog box.

2. In the **Load/Save** dialog box, click inside the text box, and then select the range in your worksheet with the saved model. For example, A11:A15.

3. Click **Load**. Excel loads the parameters saved in the selected range in the Solver Parameters dialog box.

Solver Reports

There are three types of reports you can create from the Solver Results dialog box:

- **Answer**: This report lists the result and the variable cells with their original values, final values, and any constraints used as parameters.
- **Sensitivity**: This report shows how sensitive an optimal solution is to changes in the formulas behind the objective cell and constraints.
- **Limits**: This report displays the values for the objective and variable cells, the lower and upper limits, and the results. The lower limit is the lowest value the variable cells can have while still meeting the constraints. The upper limit represents the highest value that will do this.

To generate a report, in the Solver Results dialog box, select one or more of the reports in the **Reports** list box before clicking **OK**.

You can generate one or all of the reports, as the Reports list box allows you to select more than one item on the list. When you click **OK**, Excel will generate the selected reports in separate worksheets, adding them to the beginning of the workbook.

Chapter 8

Analyze Data Dynamically with PivotTables and PivotCharts

This chapter will cover the following:

- Creating PivotTables with the Quick Analysis tool.

- Creating a Recommended PivotTable.

- Manually creating a PivotTable.

- Filtering, sorting, and formatting PivotTables.

- Creating a PivotChart.

There are different ways you can create pivot tables in Excel. We will focus here on the different methods you can use to create PivotTables, including how to generate pivot charts from the pivoted data. An Excel PivotTable is a powerful tool that lets you dynamically summarize, calculate, and analyze large data sets from different perspectives.

There are several methods for creating a new PivotTable in Excel:

- **Quick Analysis tool**: This option auto-generates a PivotTable for you. When you select all the cells in your data list and click the Quick Analysis tool on the Tables tab, you get a list of pre-designed PivotTables for your data from which you can select. When you select one, Excel inserts the PivotTable in a new worksheet.

- **Recommended PivotTables button**: This option auto-generates a PivotTable for you. When you select one cell in your data list and click the Recommended PivotTables button on the Insert tab, you get a list of recommended PivotTables from which you can select. When you select one, Excel inserts the PivotTable in a new worksheet.

- **PivotTable button**: This option enables you to create a PivotTable manually. When you select one cell in your data list and click the PivotTable button on the Insert tab, Excel opens the Create PivotTable dialog box where you specify your data source and location of the PivotTable before manually selecting the fields to use from the data.

Preparing Your Data

Some preparation is required to get a data list ready for a PivotTable. The source data used for a PivotTable needs to be organized as a list or converted to an Excel table (this is recommended, although not essential).

A few steps to prepare the source data for a PivotTable:

1. The data should have column headings in a single row on top.
2. Remove any temporary totals or summaries not part of the core data.
3. The data cannot have empty rows. So, delete any empty rows.

4. Ensure you do not have any extraneous data surrounding the list.

5. You may also want to convert the range to an Excel table (but this is optional).

	A	B	C	D	E	F	G	H
1	Employee	Product	Customer	Order Date	Ship City	Item Cost	No. of Items	Total Cost
2	Ross Grant	Cora Fabric Chair	Acme LTD	11/24/2022	Las Vegas	$475.00	20	$9,500.00
3	Jan Kotas	Lukah Leather Chair	Elgin Homes	05/13/2022	New York	$345.00	9	$3,105.00
4	Mae Stevens	Habitat Oken Console Table	Mecury Builders	04/28/2022	Las Vegas	$36.00	28	$1,008.00
5	Jesse Garza	Hygena Fabric Chair	Infinity Homes	11/06/2022	Portland	$407.00	23	$9,361.00
6	Ross Grant	Harley Fabric Cuddle Chair	Elgin Homes	07/16/2022	New York	$803.00	20	$16,060.00
7	Jan Kotas	Windsor 2 Seater Cuddle Chair	B&B Seaside	04/27/2023	Denver	$302.00	8	$2,416.00
8	Mae Stevens	Fabric Chair	B&B Seaside	06/26/2022	Los Angelas	$425.00	11	$4,675.00
9	Laura Giussani	Verona 1 Shelf Telephone Table	Home Designers	04/07/2022	Milwaukee	$282.00	8	$2,256.00
10	Ross Grant	Floral Fabric Tub Chair	Acorn USA	08/17/2022	Memphis	$158.00	2	$316.00
11	Jan Kotas	Fabric Chair in a Box	Infinity Homes	04/20/2023	Portland	$857.00	28	$23,996.00
12	Mae Stevens	Slimline Console Table	Apex Homes	11/01/2022	Chicago	$534.00	29	$15,486.00
13	Loren Pratt	Collection Martha Fabric Wingback Chair	Empire Homes	09/24/2023	Boise	$137.00	15	$2,055.00
14	Loren Pratt	Slimline Console Table	Apex Homes	04/15/2023	Chicago	$433.00	16	$6,928.00
15	Loren Pratt	Fabric Wingback Chair	Express Builders	09/03/2022	Miami	$210.00	2	$420.00
16	Loren Pratt	Fabric Chair in a Box - Denim Blue	Impressive Homes	04/23/2022	Seattle	$634.00	14	$8,876.00
17	Loren Pratt	Tessa Fabric Chair	Acorn USA	02/10/2023	Memphis	$252.00	23	$5,796.00
18	Robert Zare	Collection Bradley Riser Recline Fabric Chair	Northern Contractors	01/05/2022	Salt Lake City	$281.00	5	$1,405.00
19	Jesse Garza	Fabric Wingback Chair	Home Designers	05/15/2023	Milwaukee	$405.00	30	$12,150.00
20	Mae Stevens	Tessa Fabric Chair	Infinity Homes	05/11/2023	Portland	$472.00	5	$2,360.00
21	Ross Grant	Fabric Tub Chair	Orion Spaces	03/29/2023	Chicago	$206.00	9	$1,854.00
22	Ross Grant	Harley Fabric Cuddle Chair	Elgin Homes	08/15/2023	Miami	$247.00	18	$4,446.00
23	Loren Pratt	New Paolo Manual Recliner Chair	B&B Seaside	01/02/2022	Denver	$778.00	19	$14,782.00

Original data

Once the data has been prepared, you can now create a PivotTable.

Creating a PivotTable with the Quick Analysis Tool

Using the Quick Analysis tool, you can quickly create a pivot table for your data list in Excel. If you're not that familiar with creating PivotTables, but you have an idea of want you want to summarize, the Quick Analysis tool will recommend a series of pre-designed options from which you can choose.

Follow the steps below to create a PivotTable from the Quick Analysis tool:

1. Select all the data in your data list (including the headings).

    If you have assigned a range name to your data list, you can select the whole list by selecting the name from the Name box dropdown menu.

2. The Quick Analysis tool appears on the lower right of the selection. Click the **Quick Analysis** tool to open the Quick Analysis palette.

3. Click the **Tables** tab to display various PivotTable options for your data.

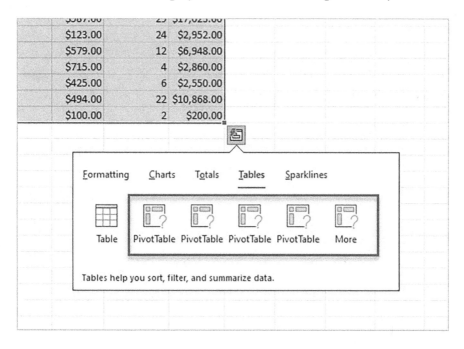

4. To see a preview of each PivotTable option, hover over each button. Excel displays a live preview of the type of PivotTable that option will generate (with your data).

5. View previews to identify the option you want, then click its button to generate. For this example, we've selected the second PivotTable option to generate a PivotTable where **Total Cost** is summed for each **Employee**.

Excel generates the PivotTable in a new worksheet (inserted in front of the worksheet with the source data). You can rename and move this worksheet to a different part of your workbook.

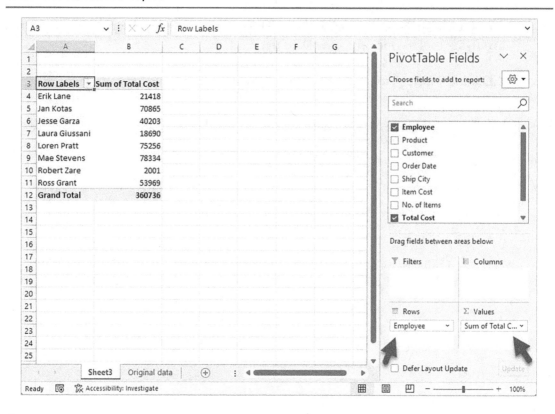

Remarks:

- When you select any area in the new PivotTable, Excel displays the **PivotTable Fields** pane on the right side of the worksheet window. The **PivotTable Analyze** and **Design** contextual tabs are also displayed on the ribbon. These contextual tabs provide several tools and commands for modifying and formatting the PivotTable, just as you would if you had created it manually.

- On some occasions, Excel may not be able to suggest PivotTable options with the Data Analysis tool, particularly if it can't analyze the data due to how it is structured. When this happens, on the Tables tab of the Quick Analysis palette, a single blank PivotTable button will be displayed after the Table button. You can click that button to manually create your PivotTable. We will cover how to manually create a PivotTable later in this chapter.

Creating a Recommended PivotTable

Another way to create a pivot table is by using the **Recommended PivotTables** command on the ribbon. This method is even faster than using the Quick Analysis tool (as long as you have prepared the data list with column headings as described earlier in this chapter).

Follow the steps below to use this method to create a PivotTable:

1. Click anywhere within the data list for which you want to create a new PivotTable.

2. On the **Insert** tab, in the **Tables** group, click the **Recommended PivotTables** button.

Excel displays the **Recommended PivotTables** pane on the right side of the window with several PivotTable options for your data. Scroll down the list to view all recommended PivotTable options.

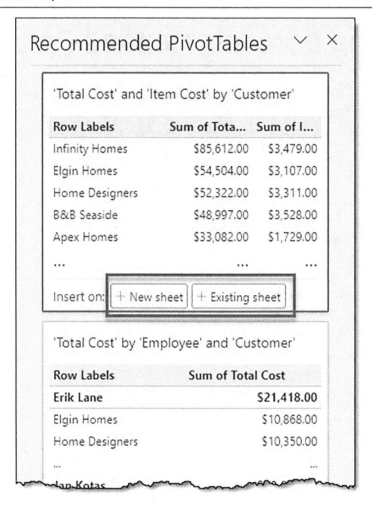

3. After identifying a PivotTable you want from the recommended list, do one of the following:

- Select the **New sheet** button to create the PivotTable in a new worksheet in the current workbook.

  Or

- Select the **Existing sheet** button to add the PivotTable to the current worksheet. Excel will prompt you to select where the PivotTable should be placed in the current sheet.

4. Clear the fields in the **PivotTable Fields** pane that you don't want to include in the summary. In the example below, the **Item Cost** field was cleared so that the PivotTable only showed the sum of Total Cost per Customer.

When you select the PivotTable on the worksheet, Excel displays the **PivotTable Fields** pane on the right side of the window and the **PivotTable Analyze** and **Design** contextual tabs on the ribbon.

If none of the Recommended PivotTables are suitable for your requirements, create the PivotTable manually.

Creating a PivotTable Manually

To create a PivotTable:

1. Select any cell in your range or table.

2. On the **Insert** tab, in the **Tables** group, click the **PivotTable** button.

   Excel displays the **PivotTable from table or range** dialog box.

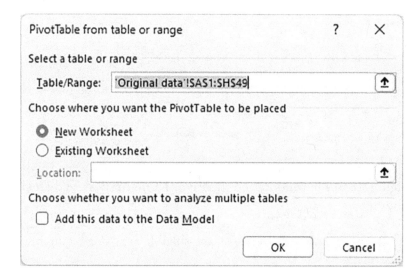

3. **Select the table/range**: Excel will attempt to figure out the table or range you want to use for your PivotTable and insert the reference in the **Table/Range** box. If this is inaccurate, you can manually select the range by clicking the Expand Dialog button (up arrow) on the box.

4. Select where you want to place the PivotTable. The default location is in a new worksheet. Having your PivotTable on a separate worksheet from your source data is best. Thus, select the **New Worksheet** option if it's not already selected.

5. Click **OK**.

Excel creates a new worksheet with a PivotTable placeholder in the worksheet area and the PivotTable Fields pane on the right side of the window.

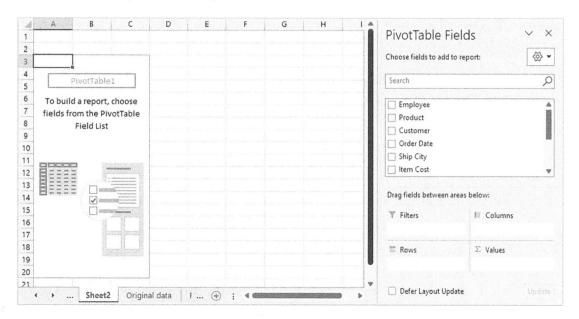

Selecting PivotTable Fields

The PivotTable Fields pane has four areas where you can place fields:

- **Filters**: The fields added here act as filters at the top of the report that enable you to display values in the PivotTable based on different criteria.

- **Columns**: The fields placed in this area are displayed as column labels in the PivotTable.

- **Rows**: The fields placed in this area become row labels (or row headings) of the PivotTable.

- **Values**: These fields are aggregated as numeric values in the PivotTable.

To add a field to your PivotTable, select the checkbox next to the field name in the PivotTable Fields pane. When you select fields, they are added to their default areas. Nonnumeric fields are added to the **Rows** area. Date and time fields are added to the **Columns** area. Numeric fields are added to the **Values** area.

You can also drag fields from the list to one of the four areas. To move a field from one area to another, you can drag it there.

To remove a field from an area, click the dropdown arrow on the field and select **Remove Field** on the shortcut menu. You can also clear the checkbox for the field in the fields list or drag it out of the box and drop it back on the fields list.

Example

In this example, let's say we want a summary of our data that shows the total spent by each Customer.

Do the following to add fields to the PivotTable placeholder generated previously:

1. Select the **Customer** field on the list to add it to the **Rows** box. The PivotTable will also be updated with the list of customers as row headings.

2. Select the **Total Cost** field to add it to the **Values** box.

The PivotTable will now be updated with the **Sum of Total Cost** for each Customer.

3	Row Labels	Sum of Total Cost
4	Acme LTD	13226
5	Acorn USA	13292
6	Apex Homes	33082
7	B&B Seaside	48997
8	Elgin Homes	54504
9	Empire Homes	9355
10	Express Builders	11004
11	Home Designers	52322
12	Impressive Homes	14775
13	Infinity Homes	85612
14	Mecury Builders	17760
15	Northern Contractors	2001
16	Orion Spaces	4806
17	**Grand Total**	360736

So, as you can see in the image above, we have been able to get a quick summary of our data with just a few clicks. If we had hundreds of thousands of records, this task could have taken many hours to accomplish manually.

We can add more values to the table by dragging them to the **Values** area from the fields list.

For example, to add the total number of items bought per customer, select **No. of Items** on the list or drag it to the **Values** box.

Excel adds the **Sum of No. of Items** for each customer to the PivotTable, as shown in the image below.

The order in which you enter the fields in the Values area affects how Excel organizes the columns in the PivotTable. You can move fields up or down in the Values area by dragging or using the **Move Up/Move Down** commands on the shortcut menu displayed when you select a field in the area.

Row Labels	Sum of No. of Items	Sum of Total Cost
Acme LTD	43	13226
Acorn USA	53	13292
Apex Homes	73	33082
B&B Seaside	88	48997
Elgin Homes	123	54504
Empire Homes	40	9355
Express Builders	14	11004
Home Designers	94	52322
Impressive Homes	31	14775
Infinity Homes	143	85612
Mecury Builders	52	17760
Northern Contractors	7	2001
Orion Spaces	33	4806
Grand Total	**794**	**360736**

To view the summary from the perspective of **Products**, i.e., the total number of items sold and the total cost for each product, drag the **Product** field to the Rows area and then drag both **Total Cost** and **No. of Items** in the **Values** area.

To view the summary from the perspective of **Employees**, place **Employee** in the Rows box, and **No. of Items** and **Total Cost** in the Values box.

Here we see the data summarised by Employee, i.e., how many items each employee sold and the revenue generated.

Row Labels	Sum of No. of Items	Sum of Total Cost
Erik Lane	40	21418
Jan Kotas	110	70865
Jesse Garza	105	40203
Laura Giussani	26	18690
Loren Pratt	181	75256
Mae Stevens	176	78334
Robert Zare	7	2001
Ross Grant	149	53969
Grand Total	**794**	**360736**

To see the number of items sold per city, place **Ship City** in the Rows area and **No. of Items** in the Values area.

	Row Labels	Sum of No. of Items
3		
4	Boise	40
5	Chicago	106
6	Denver	45
7	Las Vegas	95
8	Los Angeles	43
9	Memphis	53
10	Miami	44
11	Milwaukee	94
12	New York	93
13	Portland	143
14	Salt Lake City	7
15	Seattle	31
16	**Grand Total**	**794**

Summarizing Data by Date

To display the columns split into years, drag a date field into the Columns area, for example, Order Date. The PivotTable tool will automatically generate PivotTable fields for Quarters and Years. Once these fields have been generated, remove the Order Date field from the Columns area. Then drag the Quarter or Year field into the Columns area (depending on which one you want to use for your summary).

To display the row headings by date, place **Order Date** (or your date field) in the Rows area.

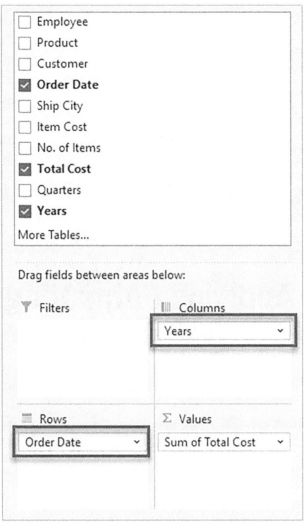

Excel displays the following results.

Sum of Total Cost	Column Labels ▾		
Row Labels ▾	2022	2023	Grand Total
Jan	39569	7772	47341
Feb		22819	22819
Mar	5502	1854	7356
Apr	22724	57618	80342
May	3105	14510	17615
Jun	24021	596	24617
Jul	16060		16060
Aug	316	12141	12457
Sep	42763	9615	52378
Oct	16752		16752
Nov	34347	9756	44103
Dec	18896		18896
Grand Total	224055	136681	360736

As you can see, we can dynamically change how we want to view our data with just a few clicks.

Applying Formatting

You can apply formatting to the appropriate columns when you're happy with your summary. For example, to change values in the report to the Currency format, select the cells in the report and apply the **Currency** format (**Home** > **Numbers** > **Currency**).

The good thing about PivotTables is that you can explore different types of summaries with the PivotTable without changing the source data. If you make a mistake that you can't figure out how to undo, you can simply delete the PivotTable worksheet and recreate it in a new worksheet.

Filtering and Sorting PivotTables

Sometimes, you may want to limit what is displayed in a PivotTable. You can sort and filter a PivotTable similar to a range or table.

Filtering a PivotTable with Slicers

An Excel Slicer is a graphical tool for filtering the data in your PivotTable. A Slicer gives you a visual indication of which items are displayed or hidden in your PivotTable.

Instead of filtering the data using the AutoFilter buttons attached to row and column labels, you can use slicers, which offer a better visual representation. Slicers are floating objects on the worksheet which can be moved around. You can insert multiple slicers to filter a PivotTable using multiple fields.

To filter your PivotTable with a slicer, select any field in the PivotTable to display the PivotTable Analyze contextual tab. On the ribbon, click the **PivotTable Analyze** tab, and in the Filter group, select **Insert Slicer**.

Excel displays the **Insert Slicers** dialog box listing all the fields you can use to filter the PivotTable.

In the Insert Slicers dialog box, select the fields for which you want to display a slicer and click **OK**. Excel adds a slicer for each selected field in the worksheet.

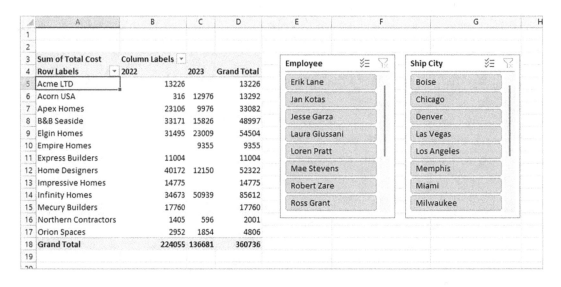

A slicer displays the values from the PivotTable field it represents. When you select a value in a slicer, the other values are deselected, indicating which value is used to filter the PivotTable. You can toggle selected values on or off by clicking them again. The values deselected or greyed out do not appear in the PivotTable.

To select multiple items, hold down the Ctrl key as you click the values in the slicer. To select multiple values in sequence, select the first value, hold down the Shift key, and select the last value. Excel selects the two values and all values between them.

You can also select multiple items by enabling the **Multi-Select** button on the slicer's title bar. With Multi-Select enabled, Excel adds additional selections to the filter instead of replacing the original selection. To clear the filter, click the **Clear Filter** button on the slicer's title bar.

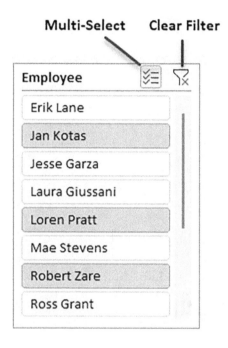

As you select values in the slicer, Excel displays the filtered PivotTable in real time, only showing list entries associated with the selected value(s) in the slicer. In the example below, the PivotTable was filtered to only show customer orders processed by employee Erik Lane.

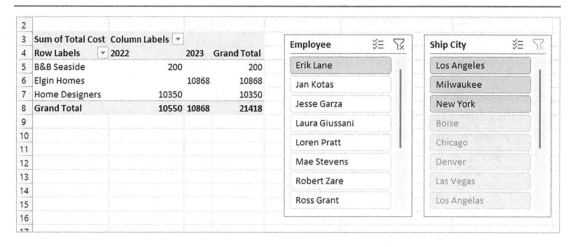

When you've finished filtering the values, you can clear the slicer filter and delete the slicer from the worksheet.

-💡-**Tip** To change the formatting of a slicer, select the slicer to display the **Slicer** context tab on the Excel ribbon. You can select different styles in the **Slicer Styles** group. In the **Arrange** group, you have commands that enable you to move and arrange groups of slicers.

Applying a Quick Filter with AutoFilter

To apply a quick filter to a PivotTable, do the following:

1. Select the AutoFilter button on the Row Labels header.

    The shortcut menu provides a list of the row headings in your PivotTable. You can select/deselect items on this list to limit the data displayed in the PivotTable.

2. Clear the **Select All** checkbox.

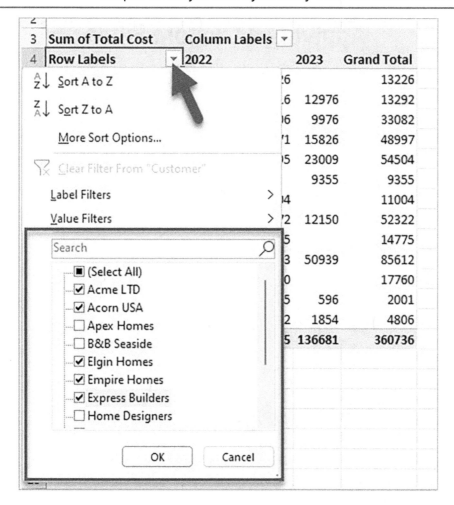

3. Scroll through the list and manually select the items you want to display in the PivotTable.

4. Click **OK**.

The PivotTable will now show only the selected columns.

Excel indicates that a PivotTable is filtered by placing a filter indicator on the AutoFilter of the Row Labels or Column Labels header. There will also be a filter indicator next to the filtered field's name in the PivotTable Fields pane.

Applying a Custom Filter

You can also use the **Label Filters** and **Value Filters** menu commands to apply a custom filter to your PivotTable. To use a conditional expression for your filter, click the AutoFilter button on the Row Labels or Column Labels header of the PivotTable.

Example

Let's say in our example, we want to display only the rows that contain "Homes" as part of the row label.

Follow the steps below to apply the custom filter:

1. Click the AutoFilter button on the Row Labels header of the PivotTable.

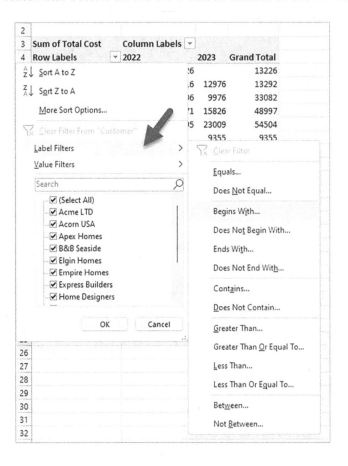

2. On the dropdown menu, select **Label Filter** > **Begins With**.

Excel displays the Label Filter dialog box.

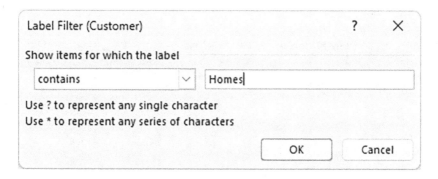

3. Ensure "contains" is selected in the dropdown list box.

4. Enter "Homes in the criteria box.

5. Click **OK**.

Excel applies the filter to the report using the condition you have set.

Sum of Total Cost	Column Labels		
Row Labels	2022	2023	Grand Total
Apex Homes	23106	9976	33082
Elgin Homes	31495	23009	54504
Empire Homes		9355	9355
Impressive Homes	14775		14775
Infinity Homes	34673	50939	85612
Grand Total	104049	93279	197328

Clearing a Filter

To clear a filter, do the following:

1. Click the AutoFilter button on the **Row Labels** header.
2. On the dropdown menu, select **Clear Filter From [*Field Name*]**.
3. Click **OK**.

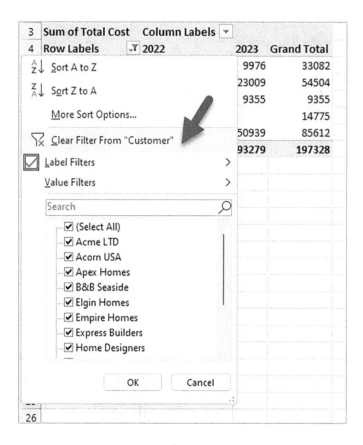

Sorting PivotTable Data

To arrange the order of the data in a PivotTable, use the same sorting methods you would use for a range or table.

1. Click the AutoFilter button on the column named **Row Labels**.

2. On the dropdown menu, select **Sort A to Z** (to sort in ascending order) or **Sort Z to A** (to sort in descending order). If your column headings are dates, you'll get **Sort Oldest to Newest** (for ascending) and **Sort Newest to Oldest** (for descending).

Creating PivotCharts

Another way to present your PivotTable data is by using charts. My *Excel 2022 Basics* book covered creating, editing, and formatting regular Excel charts. Here we will focus on generating charts from PivotTables. A PivotChart in Excel is a chart based on a PivotTable. Hence, instead of manually summarizing your data before creating a regular Excel chart, generate a PivotTable on which your base the chart. This process enables you to create a dynamic chart just like the source PivotTable.

To create a PivotChart from a PivotTable, do the following:

1. Select any cell in the PivotTable. On the **Insert** tab, in the **Charts** group, select **PivotChart**.

    Excel opens the **Insert Chart** dialog box, which allows you to select the type and subtype of the pivot chart you want to create.

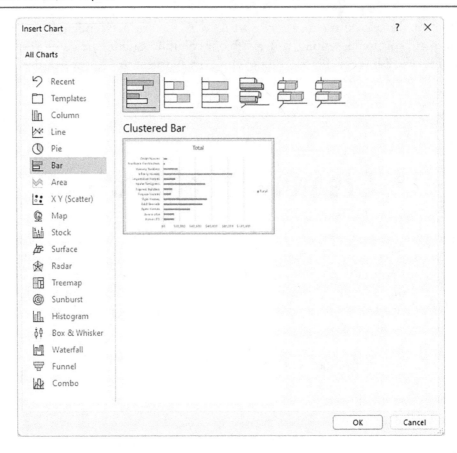

2. On the Insert Chart dialog box, select the type and subtype of the chart you want to create and click **OK**.

    Excel inserts an embedded PivotChart in the worksheet with the PivotTable used as the data source.

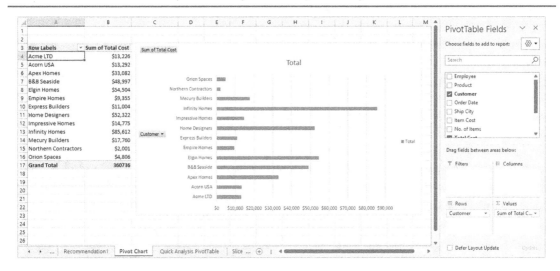

Tip To move the chart around the window, hover over the chart until the mouse pointer changes to a crosshair, then click and drag the chart to any part of the screen you want.

Sorting and Filtering PivotCharts

There are several ways you can sort and filter a PivotChart. You can filter or sort the chart using the source PivotTable or elements on the chart itself.

Sorting Axis Labels

To sort axis labels on the chart, sort the Row Labels header in the source PivotTable:

1. On the PivotTable, click the AutoFilter button on the **Row Labels** header.

2. On the dropdown menu, select **Sort A to Z** (to sort in ascending order) or **Sort Z to A** (to sort in descending order). If axis values are dates, you'll get **Sort Oldest to Newest** (for ascending) and **Sort Newest to Oldest** (for descending).

You can also use Field Buttons on the PivotChart to sort and filter the chart as described below.

Filtering a PivotChart

After generating a new PivotChart, you'll see Axis Field Buttons representing fields on the chart. You can use these dropdown buttons to AutoFilter or AutoSort the PivotChart in the same way you can with the PivotTable.

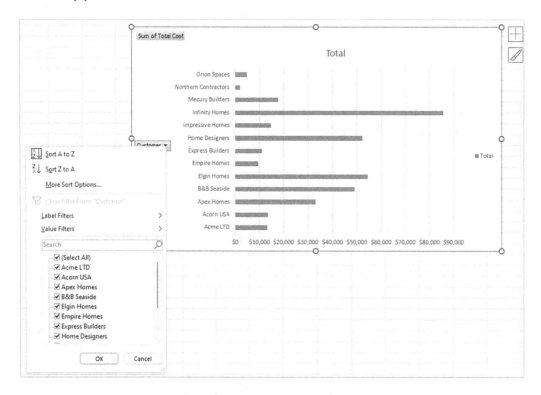

The example above has the **Customer** field button on the chart representing the y-axis labels.

For instance, to exclude some customers from the chart, do the following:

1. Click the **Customer** field button, and on the shortcut menu, clear **Select All**.

2. On the shortcut menu, select the values you want to display in the PivotChart individually.

3. Click **OK**.

Excel filters the PivotChart to only display the selected names.

Note You can also sort the PivotChart using the shortcut menu on an Axis Field Button.

To hide the Field Buttons on the chart, for example, if you want to print the chart without the buttons, do the following:

1. On the ribbon, click the **PivotChart Analyze** tab.

2. In the **Show/Hide** group, click **Field Buttons** (click the button's image rather than its dropdown arrow). You can toggle this button to show or hide the field buttons on the chart.

Customizing a PivotChart

When you select the PivotChart, three additional tabs appear on the ribbon, **PivotChart Analyze**, **Design**, and **Format**. You can use commands on these tabs to modify the format and design of the PivotChart. For example, the **Add Chart Elements** button on the **Design** tab enables you to add or remove elements from the PivotChart. Among many elements, you can add or remove Data Labels, Axis Titles, Gridlines, and a Legend.

Adding Data Labels

To add Data Labels to your PivotChart, do the following:

1. Select the PivotChart to display its related contextual tabs.

2. On the **Design** tab, in the **Chart Layouts** group, select **Add Chart Elements** > **Data Labels** > **Outside End**.

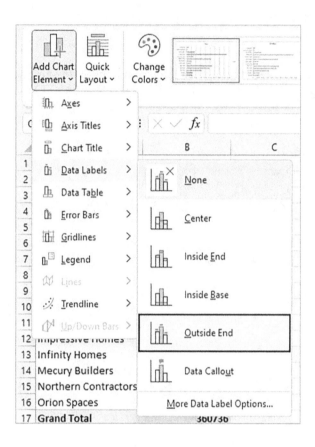

Excel adds data labels to the bars on the chart.

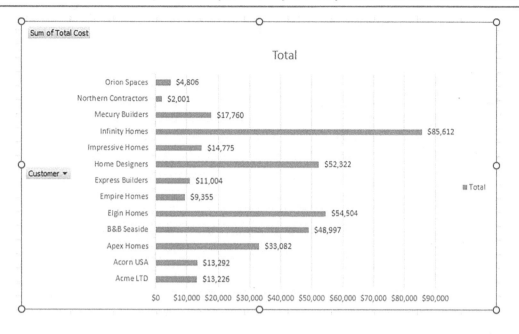

Adding Axis Titles

You can add axis titles to the left and bottom of the chart. The left side is the y-axis, and the bottom is the x-axis.

1. Select the PivotChart to display its related contextual tabs.

2. On the **Design** tab, in the **Chart Layouts** group, select **Axis Titles > Primary Vertical**.

Excel adds a title to the y-axis of the chart. You can double-click the label and edit the title.

Editing the Chart Title

To change the Chart Title, you can simply select it and type in the title. Alternatively, you can set the name to a cell reference in your worksheet to display the text in that cell.

To change the chart title to a value in cell A1 of the worksheet, do the following:

1. Enter the text value in cell A1.

2. Select the **Chart Title** element on the chart.

3. In the formula bar, type "=" and select cell A1 in the worksheet area. Excel enters = **'Pivot Chart'!$A$1** in the formula bar where 'Pivot Chart' represents the name of your worksheet.

The title of the PivotChart will now show the text entered in cell A1.

Quick Chart Layouts

Quick layouts provide several layout options for your chart that add or remove certain chart elements. You can use layout options to reposition the Legend, add Axis Titles, and add Data Labels.

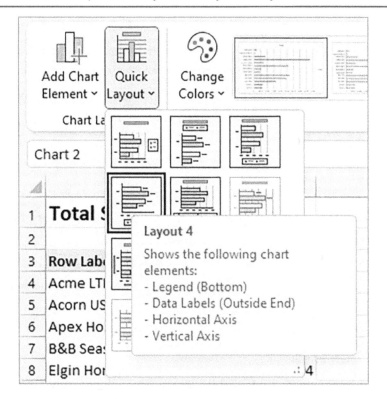

To change the layout of your chart, do the following:

1. Select the chart.

2. On the **Design** tab, in the **Chart Layouts** group, click **Quick Layout**.

3. Select one of the layout options from the gallery. To preview a layout option without selecting it, hover over it, and Excel displays a preview of how your chart will look with that layout option.

Chart Styles

The **Design** tab shows up on the ribbon when you select a PivotChart. On this tab, you have various **Chart Styles** you can choose from to change your chart's overall look and color.

To change your chart style to one of the predefined styles, do the following:

1. Click the chart to select it.

2. On the **Design** contextual tab, in the **Chart Styles** group, click the **More** button (dropdown arrow) and select one of the styles from the gallery.

3. You can hover over each style to preview how your chart will look with that style.

4. When you identify a suitable option, select it to apply it to your chart.

To change the color of the plot area:

1. Click a blank space in the chart's plot area to select the whole area.

2. On the **Format** tab, in the **Shape Styles** group, click the **More** button to expand the styles gallery.

3. Hover over each style to see a preview of what your chart would look like if selected.

4. When you identify a suitable option, select it to apply it to your chart.

To change the colors of the bars on the graph, do the following:

1. Click the chart to select it.

2. On the **Design** tab, in the **Chart Styles** group, click **Change Colors**.

3. You can hover over each color combination on the palette to preview the result on your chart.

4. When you identify an option you want, select it to apply it to your chart.

Moving a PivotChart

To move the chart to another worksheet, do the following:

1. Select the PivotChart.

2. On the ribbon, select **PivotChart Analyze > Actions > Move Chart**.

   Excel displays the **Move Chart** dialog box.

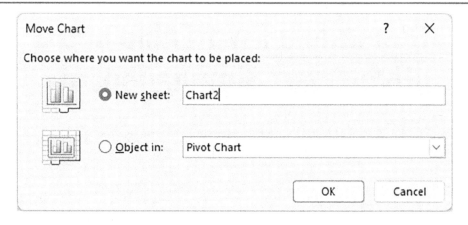

3. Select **New sheet,** and in the corresponding text box, you can accept the default name provided for the new worksheet or type in another name of your choosing.

4. Click **OK** when you're done.

Excel moves the chart to a new worksheet.

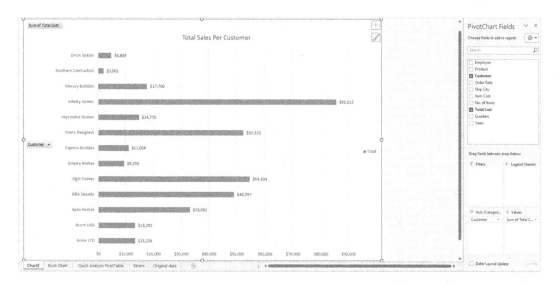

Generate a PivotTable and a PivotChart Simultaneously

You can generate a PivotTable and a PivotChart simultaneously from your table or data list instead of creating them separately.

To generate a PivotTable and PivotChart together, do the following:

1. Click anywhere in the data list.
2. On the **Insert** tab, click the dropdown arrow on the **PivotChart** button.
3. Select **PivotChart & PivotTable** from the dropdown menu on the command button.
4. In the Create PivotTable dialog box, click the **OK** button.

Excel will create a new worksheet with the placeholders for a PivotTable and a PivotChart.

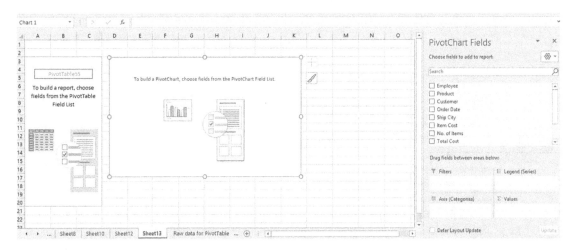

In the **PivotChart Fields** pane, select the fields to display in your PivotTable and PivotChart. As you select the fields you want for the chart in the PivotChart Fields pane, the PivotTable and PivotChart are updated simultaneously.

Follow the steps described in the sections titled **Creating PivotTables Manually** and **Creating PivotCharts** in this chapter to finalize the PivotTable and PivotChart.

Chapter 9

Protect Workbooks, Worksheets, and Ranges

This chapter covers how to:

- Password-protect your Excel file.

- Set different access levels for your workbook with passwords.

- Protect your workbook structure from unauthorized changes.

- Protect individual worksheets within a workbook.

- Protect specific ranges within a worksheet.

Excel provides security at different levels of granularity. You can protect workbooks, worksheets, ranges, and individual cells from unauthorized access and changes. This chapter will cover the various methods you can use to protect your workbook.

⚠ Important

Before you protect your workbook with a password, ensure that you've got the password written down and stored in a safe place where it can be retrieved if necessary. Microsoft does not provide any methods to access a password-protected Excel file where the password has been lost. Without an advanced password-cracking tool, it is impossible to gain access to an Excel file that has been password-protected if the password has been forgotten.

How to set a password for your Excel workbook:

To set a password on your Excel workbook, do the following:

1. From the Excel ribbon, select **File** > **Info** > **Protect Document** > **Encrypt with Password**.

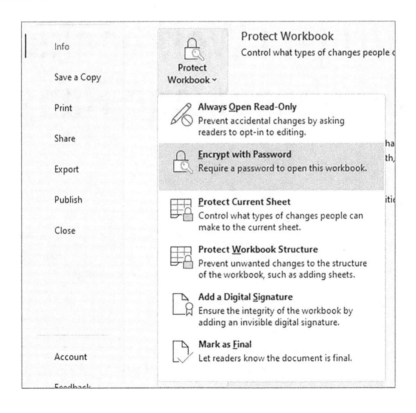

2. At the prompt, enter your password, then confirm it.

3. Click **OK** after confirming the password.

4. Save and close the workbook.

5. When you reopen the workbook, Excel will prompt you for the password.

That's it! You now have a password protected file.

Removing a Password from an Excel Workbook

Sometimes, you may want to remove a password from an Excel workbook. Setting a password encrypts the workbook, so you'll need to remove the encryption. Carry out the following steps to remove the password.

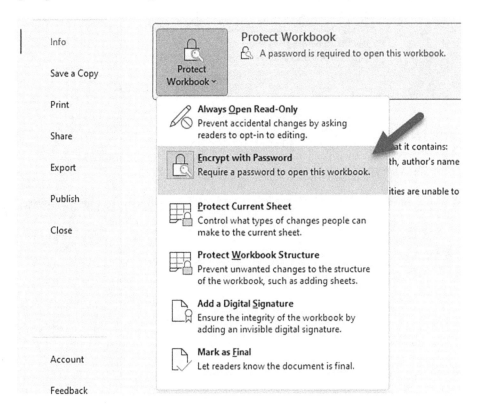

1. Open the workbook and enter the password in the **Password** box.

2. Select **File** > **Info** > **Protect Workbook** > **Encrypt with Password**.

   Excel displays the Encrypt Document dialog box.

3. Delete the contents of the **Password** box.

4. Click **OK**.

5. Save the workbook and close it.

When you reopen the workbook, Excel will not challenge you for a password.

Set Different Access Levels

The password protection method described in the previous section enables you to quickly protect your Excel workbook from unauthorized access with a password. However, it does not provide a way to set different access levels, like **read-only** and **read-write** access. To set different access levels with passwords, you need to use the older method to save the file with a different name and insert the passwords during the process. This method allows you to set separate passwords for opening and modifying the file.

Note Only use this method (over the encryption method described in the previous section) if you want to create different access levels for different groups of users.

To set different passwords for opening and modifying an Excel file, do the following:

1. On the ribbon, select **File** > **Save As** (or **Save a Copy** if your workbook is on OneDrive and AutoSave is set to **On**).

2. Click the **More options** link (directly under the file type box). Excel opens the **Save As** dialog box.

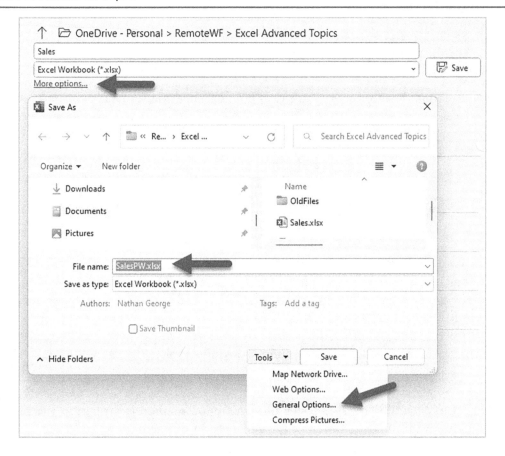

3. In the **Save As** dialog box, click the **Tools** button and select **General Options** from the menu.

   Excel displays the **General Options** dialog box, which enables you to set one password for opening the workbook and another for modifying the workbook.

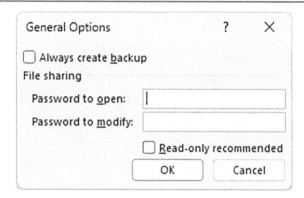

4. Enter different passwords in the **Password to modify** and **Password to open** boxes, and then click **OK**.

5. Excel will display two **Confirm Password** prompts. Re-enter the password you entered in **Password to open** and **Password to modify** to confirm them.

6. In the **Save As** dialog box, in the **File name** field, enter a new name for the workbook and click **Save**. You must save the file with a new name, as Excel will not allow you to save it with the current name.

7. Close and reopen the workbook (the file saved with the new name). This time Excel will challenge you with a prompt for a password to open the workbook. Enter the password and click **OK**.

8. Excel will display another password prompt for Write Access to the workbook. Enter the Write Access password in the **Password** field and click **OK** (this is the password set in the **Password to modify** box).

To open and modify the workbook, you need both passwords. For read-only access, you enter the password to open at the first prompt and then click the **Read Only** button at the second prompt.

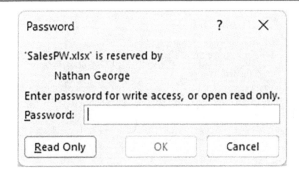

Removing the Passwords Set in General Options

There may be situations when you want to remove file protection and make the file accessible to all users. To remove the passwords set in General Options, you can delete them from General Options and save the file again.

Do the following to remove the passwords:

1. Open the Excel file with the current passwords.

2. Select **File** > **Save As** (or **Save a Copy** if your file is saved on OneDrive).

3. Click the **More options** link (directly under the file type box).

    Excel opens the **Save As** dialog box.

4. In the **Save As** dialog box, select **Tools** > **General Options**. Excel displays the **General Options** dialog box where you entered the passwords.

5. Clear the passwords from the **Password to modify** and **Password to open** boxes, and click **OK** to dismiss the dialog box.

6. In the **Save As** dialog box, click **Save** to save the file.

    If you use the same file name, Excel will display a message asking if you want to replace the current file.

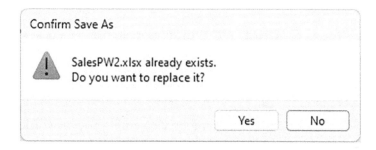

7. Select **Yes** to replace the file or **No** to go back to the Save As dialog and change the name.

8. Close the workbook and reopen it. It will no longer prompt you for a password.

Protect the Workbook Structure

You can protect your workbook structure with a password to prevent other users from adding, moving, deleting, renaming, hiding, or viewing hidden worksheets. Protecting the workbook structure differs from protecting an Excel file or worksheet with a password. When you protect your workbook structure, the file is still accessible to everyone with access, but they can't change the workbook's structure. This type of protection does not protect the data from being modified, only the workbook's structure.

To protect your workbook, carry out the following steps:

1. On the **Review** tab, in the **Protect** group, select **Protect Workbook**.

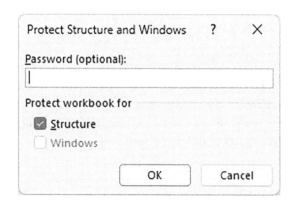

2. In the **Protect Structure and Windows** dialog, enter a password in the **Password** box.

3. Click **OK**.

4. In the **Confirm Password** dialog box, re-enter the password and click **OK**.

The **Protect Workbook** button on the Review tab will be enabled, indicating that the workbook is protected.

With the workbook protected, all the commands that involve changing the workbook's structure, like add, delete, move, or rename worksheets are disabled. To re-enable these commands, you'll need to remove the password protection.

Unprotecting the Workbook Structure

To unprotect your workbook's structure, do the following:

1. On the **Review** tab of the ribbon, in the **Protect** group, click **Protect Workbook**.

2. In the **Unprotect Workbook** dialog box, enter the password used to protect the workbook and click **OK**.

Protect Worksheets

Instead of protecting the whole workbook with a password, you could protect individual worksheets and even narrow it down to restricting certain actions within the sheet. For example, you can lock certain cells in the worksheet with formulas from being editable so that other users do not accidentally delete formulas.

In a shared workbook, users could inadvertently delete formulas as they may not be aware that some cells contain formulas rather than values. Hence, cells with formulas are often protected in shared workbooks. Another reason to protect parts of your worksheet is that you may have core data that you don't want users to change. You can protect those ranges only on the worksheet.

Worksheet protection involves two steps:

1. First, unlock the cells that you want to keep editable. If you don't take this step, all cells in the worksheet will be locked when you protect it.

2. Protect the worksheet with or without a password.

Step 1 - Unlock any cells/ranges that need to be editable:

1. Click the tab of the worksheet you want to protect. In the worksheet area, select the range(s) to be left unprotected.

-☼-**Tip** You can select multiple ranges by holding down the **Ctrl** key while selecting additional ranges.

---

2. On the **Home** tab, in the **Cells** group, select **Format** > **Format Cells**.

3. In the **Format Cells** dialog box, select the **Protection** tab and clear the **Locked** checkbox.

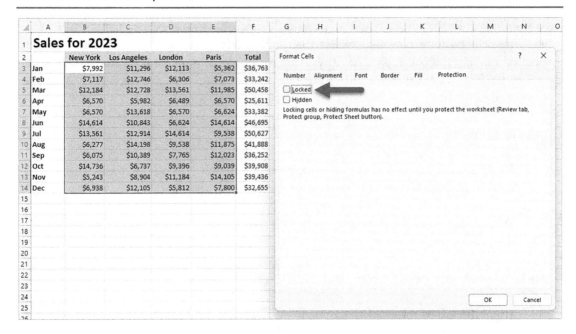

Step 2 - Protect the worksheet:

Next, you can choose specific actions that users can carry out in the worksheet.

1. On the **Review** tab, in the **Protect** group, click **Protect Sheet**.

   Excel displays the **Protect Sheet** dialog box.

2. Ensure the **Protect worksheet and contents of locked cells** setting is selected. This setting should be enabled by default.

3. In the list box, select the actions users can perform on the worksheet. For example, you could allow users to insert rows and columns, sort data, format cells, use AutoFilter, etc., among the many options on the list.

4. You can specify a password that a user will require to unprotect the sheet, but this is optional.

   You can protect the sheet without a password, but users can click the **Unprotect Sheet** button to unprotect the sheet. If you want to prevent users from doing this, enter a password in the **Password to unprotect sheet** box and click **OK**. Re-enter the password at the **Confirm Password** prompt and click **OK** to complete the action.

⚠ **Important**

If you set a password to protect your worksheet, you'll need the password whenever you want to unprotect it. Hence, it is critical that you remember your password. Ideally, you want to have it written down somewhere under lock and key for easy retrieval if needed. If the password is lost, Microsoft provides no tools to retrieve it.

Unprotect a Worksheet

In a protected worksheet, in place of the **Protect Sheet** command button on the **Review** tab, you'll see an **Unprotect Sheet** command button.

To unprotect the sheet, click the **Unprotect Sheet** button. You'll be challenged with a password prompt if it is protected with a password. Enter the password, and click **OK** to unprotect the worksheet.

Protect Specific Ranges

Excel locks all cells by default when you protect a worksheet unless you specifically unlock some cells before you enable protection (as described above). Hence, you must remove the sheet protection to access the locked parts of the sheet.

What if we have situations where we want some users to access locked ranges without removing the sheet protection?

Excel provides a solution with the **Allow Edit Ranges** command. You can password-protect specific ranges in the worksheet rather than the whole sheet. Also, if you're using a Microsoft Windows machine on a network domain, you can give specific users in your domain permission to edit ranges in a protected worksheet.

The process involves two steps:

1. Specify the ranges to be password protected.

2. Protect the worksheet.

Step 1 - Follow these steps to specify the ranges to be password protected:

1. If the worksheet is already protected, you need to unprotect the sheet first.

2. Select the worksheet you want to protect by clicking its tab at the bottom of the Excel window.

3. On the **Review** tab, in the **Protect** group, click the **Allow Edit Ranges** button. This button is only available when the worksheet is unprotected.

   Excel displays the **Allow Users to Edit Ranges** dialog box.

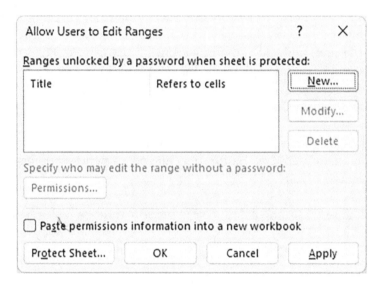

4. Click **New** to add a new range that you want editable using a password.

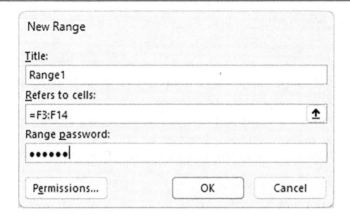

5. In the **New Range** dialog box, in the **Title** box, name the range you want to password-protect.

6. In the **Refers to cells** box, enter the cell reference of the range, starting with an equal sign (=). Alternatively, select the Collapse Dialog button (the up arrow on the right of the box) and select the range on the worksheet. Then click the Expand Dialog button to return to the New Range dialog box.

7. In the **Range password** box, enter a password that allows access to the range.

   To use domain permissions, click the **Permissions** button and follow the process to add a domain user. This button only applies to network domains with multiple user accounts.

8. Click **OK** to return to the **Allow Users to Edit Ranges** dialog box.

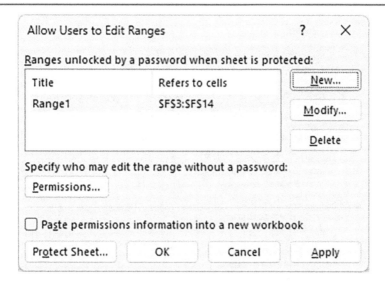

Step 2 - Protect the worksheet:

If you have closed the **Allow Users to Edit Ranges** dialog box, open it again by selecting **Review > Protect > Protect Sheet**.

1. In the **Allow Users to Edit Ranges** dialog box, select the **Protect Sheet** button.

   Excel displays the **Protect Sheet** dialog box.

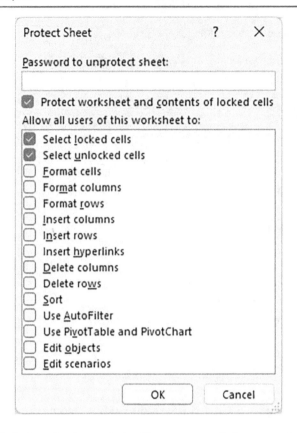

2. Accept the default selection of the **Protect worksheet and contents of locked cells** checkbox. If it is not enabled, then select it.

3. In the **Allow all users of this worksheet to** list, select the actions users can perform in the worksheet. For example, you could allow users to insert rows and columns, sort data, format cells, or use AutoFilter, among the many options on the list.

4. In the **Password to unprotect sheet** box, enter a password and click **OK**. Re-enter the password to confirm it and click **OK** again.

    As mentioned previously, the password is optional. If you don't set a password, the sheet will be protected, but any user can click the **Unprotect Sheet** button on the ribbon to unprotect the sheet.

Once a range has been protected, users will be prompted to enter the password set in Step 1 when they try to edit the range. A user will only need to enter the password once per session.

⚠ Important

Although mentioned earlier in this chapter, this is worth repeating. If you protect any part of your worksheet with a password, you'll need the password to unprotect it. Hence, it is critical that you remember your password. Ideally, you want to have it written down somewhere under lock and key for easy retrieval if needed. If you forget the password, Microsoft provides no tools to retrieve it.

More Help

Thank you for buying and reading this book. The scope of this book has been kept to a selection of practical topics relevant to real world productivity tasks you could encounter in your work business or studies. If you have any questions or comments, please contact me at **support@excelbytes.com**.

For more Excel books, visit our website:

https://www.excelbytes.com

You can also visit Excel's official online help site at:

https://support.office.com/en-gb/excel

This is a comprehensive help center for Excel. Although not an organized tutorial like this book, it is a useful resource when looking for help on a specific feature or tool in Excel. You'll also find resources like Excel templates that you can download and use as the starting basis for your worksheets.

Appendix: Keyboard Shortcuts (Excel for Windows)

The Excel ribbon comes with new shortcuts called Key Tips. To see Key Tips, press the **Alt** key when Excel is the active window.

The following table lists the most frequently used shortcuts in Excel.

Keystroke	Action
F1	Opens Excel's Help window
Ctrl+O	Open a workbook
Ctrl+W	Close a workbook
Ctrl+C	Copy
Ctrl+V	Paste
Ctrl+X	Cut
Ctrl+Z	Undo

Ctrl+B	Bold
Ctrl+S	Save a workbook
Ctrl+F1	Displays or hides the Ribbon
Delete key	Remove cell contents
Alt+H	Go to the Home tab
Alt+H, H	Choose a fill color
Alt+N	Go to the Insert tab
Alt+A	Go to the Data tab
Alt+P	Go to the Page Layout tab
Alt+H, A, then C	Center align cell contents
Alt+W	Go to the View tab
Shift+F10, or Context key	Open context menu
Alt+H, B	Add borders
Alt+H,D, then C	Delete column
Alt+M	Go to the Formula tab
Ctrl+9	Hide the selected rows
Ctrl+0	Hide the selected columns

Access Keys for Ribbon Tabs

To go directly to a tab on the Excel Ribbon, press one of the following access keys.

Action	Keystroke
Activate the Search box.	Alt+Q
Open the File page, i.e., the Backstage view.	Alt+F
Open the Home tab.	Alt+H
Open the Insert tab.	Alt+N
Open the Page Layout tab.	Alt+P
Open the Formulas tab.	Alt+M
Open the Data.	Alt+A
Open the Review.	Alt+R
Open the View.	Alt+W

To get a more comprehensive list of Excel for Windows shortcuts, press **F1** to open Excel Help and type in "Keyboard shortcuts" in the search bar.

Glossary

Absolute reference
This is a cell reference that doesn't change when you copy a formula containing the reference to another cell. For example, $A$3 means the row and column have been set to absolute.

Add-in
A different application you can add to extend the functionality of Excel. It could be from Microsoft or a third-party vendor.

Active cell
The cell that is currently selected and open for editing.

Alignment
The way a cell's contents are arranged within that cell. This could be left, centered, or right.

Argument
The input values a function requires to carry out a calculation or evaluation.

AutoCalculate
This is an Excel feature that automatically calculates and displays the summary of a selected range of figures on the status bar.

AutoComplete

This is an Excel feature that completes data entry for a range of cells based on values in other cells in the same column or row.

Backstage view

The screen you see when you click the File tab on the ribbon. It has a series of menu options to do with managing your workbook and configuring global settings in Excel.

Cell reference

The letter and number combination that represents the intersection of a column and row. For example, B10 means column B, row 10.

Chart

A visual representation of summarized worksheet data.

Conditional format

This is a format that applies only when certain criteria are met by the cell content.

Conditional formula

A conditional formula calculates a value from one of two expressions based on whether a third expression evaluates to true or false.

Delimiter

A character in a text file that is used to separate the values into columns.

Dependent

A cell with a formula that references other cells, so its value is dependent on other cells.

Dialog box launcher

In the lower-right corner of some groups on the Excel ribbon, you'll see a diagonal down-pointing arrow. When you click the arrow, it opens a dialog box containing several additional options for that group.

Digital certificate

A file with a unique string of characters that can be combined with an Excel workbook to create a verifiable signature.

Digital signature

A mathematical construct that combines a file and a digital certificate to verify the authorship of the file.

Excel table

This is a cell range that has been defined as a table in Excel. Excel adds certain attributes to the range to make it easier to manipulate the data as a table.

Fill handle

A small square on the lower right of the cell pointer. You can drag this handle to AutoFill values for other cells.

Fill series

This is the Excel functionality that allows you to create a series of values based on a starting value and any rules or intervals included.

Formula

An expression used to calculate a value.

Formula bar

This is the area just above the worksheet grid that displays the value of the active cell. This is where you enter a formula in Excel.

Function

A function is a predefined formula in Excel that just requires input values (arguments) to calculate and return a value.

Goal Seek

An analysis tool that can be used to create projections by setting the goal, and the tool calculates the input values required to meet the goals from a set number of variables.

Graph

A representation of summarized worksheet data, also known as a chart.

Live Preview

A preview of whatever task you want to perform based on your actual data. So, you get to see how your data will look if you carry out the command.

Locked cell

A locked cell cannot be modified if the worksheet is protected.

Macro

A series of instructions created from recording Excel tasks that automate Excel when replayed.

Named range

A group of cells in your worksheet given one name that can then be used as a reference.

OneDrive

This is a cloud storage service provided by Microsoft which automatically syncs your files to a remote drive, hence providing instant backups.

PivotChart

A specific kind of Excel chart related to a PivotTable. A PivotChart can be dynamically reorganized to show different views of your data, just like a PivotTable.

PivotTable

This is an Excel summary table that allows you to dynamically summarise data from different perspectives. PivotTables are highly flexible, and you can quickly adjust them depending on how you need to display your results.

Precedent

A cell that is used as a cell reference in a formula in another cell. Also, see Dependent.

Quick Access Toolbar

This is a customizable toolbar with a set of commands independent of the tab and ribbon commands currently on display.

Relative reference

Excel cell references are relative references by default. This means when copied across multiple cells, they change based on the relative position of columns and rows.

Ribbon

This is the top part of the Excel screen that contains the tabs and commands.

Scenario

An alternative set of data that you can use the compare the impact of changes in your data. This is useful when creating projections and forecasts.

Solver

An Excel add-in that enables you to create scenarios for more complex data models.

Sort

A sort means to reorder the data in a worksheet in ascending or descending order by one or more columns.

Tracer arrows

Graphical arrows that are used to indicate dependent or precedent cells.

Watch

The watch window can be used to display the contents of a cell in a separate window even when the cell is not visible on the screen.

What-If Analysis

A series of methods that can be used to determine the impact of changes on your data. This could include projections and forecasts.

Workbook

This is the Excel document itself, and it can contain one or more worksheets.

Worksheet

A worksheet is like a page in an Excel workbook.

x-axis

The horizontal axis of a chart where you could have time intervals etc.

y-axis

This is the vertical axis of a chart, which usually depicts value data.

Index

About the Author

Nathan George is a computer science graduate with several years of experience in the IT services industry in different roles, which included Excel VBA programming, Access development, Excel training, and providing end-user support to Excel power users. One of his main interests is using computers to automate tasks and increase productivity. As an author, he has written several technical and non-technical books.

.

Other Books by Author

Excel 2022 Basics

A Quick and Easy Guide to Boosting Your Productivity with Excel

Excel 2022 Basics covers all you need to get up to speed in creating Excel solutions for your data. This book covers all the features, commands, and functions you'll need for everyday Excel use in your job or home, using practical examples relevant to real-world Excel productivity tasks.

Comes with free downloadable Excel practice files for faster learning.

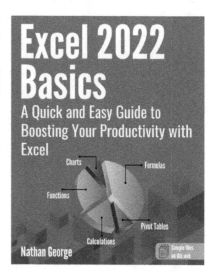

Available at Amazon:
https://www.amazon.com/dp/1915476038

Excel 2019 Macros and VBA

An Introduction to Excel Programming

Take your Excel skills to the next level with macros and Visual Basic for Applications (VBA)!

Create solutions that would have otherwise been too cumbersome or impossible to create with standard Excel commands and functions. Automate Excel for repetitive tasks and save yourself time and tedium.

With *Excel 2019 Macros and VBA,* you'll learn how to automate Excel using quick macros as well as writing VBA code. You'll learn all the VBA fundamentals to enable you to start creating your own code from scratch.

Available at Amazon:
https://www.amazon.com/dp/1916211348

For more Excel books, go to:
https://www.excelbytes.com/excel-books

Mastering Access 365

An Easy Guide to Building Efficient Databases for Managing Your Data

Has your data become too large and complex for Excel? If so, then Access may be the tool you need. Whether you're new to Access or looking to refresh your skills on this popular database application, you'll find everything you need to create efficient and robust database solutions for your data in this book.

Mastering Access 365 offers straightforward step-by-step explanations with practical examples for hands-on learning. This book covers Access for Microsoft 365 and Access 2021.

Available at Amazon:

https://www.amazon.com/dp/1916211399

www.ingramcontent.com/pod-product-compliance
Lightning Source LLC
LaVergne TN
LVHW062307060326
832902LV00013B/2094